Poetic Freedom
and
Poetic Truth

POETIC FREEDOM AND POETIC TRUTH

Chaucer, Shakespeare, Marlowe, Milton

HARRIETT HAWKINS

CLARENDON PRESS · OXFORD

Oxford University Press, Walton Street, Oxford OX2 6DP

OXFORD LONDON GLASGOW NEW YORK
TORONTO MELBOURNE WELLINGTON CAPE TOWN
IBADAN NAIROBI DAR ES SALAAM LUSAKA ADDIS ABABA
KUALA LUMPUR SINGAPORE JAKARTA HONG KONG TOKYO
DELHI BOMBAY CALCUTTA MADRAS KARACHI

ISBN 0 19 812071 0

*Printed and bound in Great Britain by
Morrison & Gibb Ltd, London and Edinburgh*

For
Genevieve Bloker Hawkins
and her daughter, Juliana

If an artist falsifies his report as to the nature of man, as to his own nature, as to the nature of his ideal of the perfect, as to the nature of his ideal of this, that or the other, of god, if god exist, of the life force, of the nature of good and evil, if good and evil exist, of the force with which he believes or disbelieves this, that or the other, of the degree in which he suffers or is made glad, if the artist falsifies his reports on these matters or on any other matter in order that he may conform to the taste of his time, to the proprieties of a sovereign, to the conveniences of a preconceived code of ethics, then that artist lies.

EZRA POUND

Give me the liberty to know, to utter, and to argue freely according to conscience, above all liberties.

MILTON

> I formed them free, and free they must remain,
> Till they enthrall themselves.

MILTON'S GOD

But each for the joy of the working, and each, in his separate star,
Shall draw the Thing as he sees It for the God of Things as they are!

KIPLING

Acknowledgements

THIS book was written while I held a generous grant from the American Council of Learned Societies. A short extract from Chapter III was published in the 'Forum' of the *PMLA*, and a slightly modified version of Chapter II has been published in *Signs: Journal of Women in Culture and Society* (Vol. 1, No. 2, December, 1975). Most of the first chapter was first presented, in lecture form, at the University of Oxford.

I am deeply grateful to R. M. Adams, J. B. Bamborough, Hugh Lloyd-Jones, and D. T. Mace, who gave me valuable criticisms of individual chapters.

Quotations follow F. N. Robinson's edition of *The Works of Geoffrey Chaucer*, revised edition, Cambridge, Mass., 1957; *The Complete Works of Shakespeare*, edited by Hardin Craig, Chicago, 1961; *The Plays of Christopher Marlowe*, edited by Roma Gill, London, 1971; *John Milton: Complete Poems and Major Prose*, edited by Merritt Y. Hughes, New York, 1957; *Five Plays by Ben Jonson* (World's Classics text modernized from the edition of Ben Jonson's *Works*, ed. C. H. Herford, and Percy and Evelyn Simpson, to which line references here refer), London, 1962; *The Poetical Works of Spenser*, edited by J. C. Smith and E. de Selincourt, London, 1965; Thomas Middleton and William Rowley, *The Changeling*, edited by N. W. Bawcutt, Cambridge, Mass., 1961; John Webster, *The Duchess of Malfi*, edited by John Russell Brown, Cambridge, Mass., 1964; John Lyly, *Campaspe*, in *Five Elizabethan Comedies*, edited by A. K. McIlwraith, London, 1959. Winnie Davin gave me the quotation from Joyce Cary on page 6.

Vassar College, 1975   H.H.

Preface

The world was all before them, where to choose . . .　　　MILTON

THEIR magnificently successful efforts to embody in poetry the truth as they knew it have given 'immortal glory among mortals' to Chaucer, Shakespeare, Milton, and some of their great contemporaries. Yet a series of major problems has been created by their insistence upon their divine right to argue freely; by their persistent refusals merely to mirror the orthodoxies of the time; and by their frequent refusals to interfere with our own freedom to 'see and know', and interpret for ourselves, the truth about human experience, as they have re-created it before us, in its infinite and disturbing variety. This book attempts to pose, though it by no means claims to solve,[1] some of the most obvious of these problems.

The first chapter, which is mainly about characters in Chaucer's *Canterbury Tales* and Shakespeare's plays, discusses 'Poetic Injustice' of various kinds. Why, instead of obeying critical orders and showing us vice punished and virtue triumphant, do major poets so frequently introduce characters who get far more suffering, or many more rewards, than their individual vices or virtues have merited? A discussion of certain characters who seem to have been created to be 'winners' and 'losers' of differing types suggests that many instances of 'poetic injustice' serve to illustrate some truth about human experience which, without them, might otherwise have been falsified, distorted, or overlooked entirely.

The second chapter focuses on works which encourage the

---

[1] Many of the problems posed in this book commonly arise in the minds of serious readers, and in masterpieces other than the ones surveyed here. Some of them are, I am convinced, insoluble; some seem deliberately built-in to the texts by the poets themselves. It therefore seems mistaken to assume that it is the business of criticism to solve problems and answer questions which the poets themselves conceive to be insoluble or leave unanswered. No claim to any definitive interpretation of the works discussed is here made or intended.

reader to take 'The Victim's Side', and so to join the author in his protests against specific forms of social, sexual, or political injustice. It is also concerned with threats to poetic liberty. For over the past several decades, there has been a serious scholarly effort to deny the poet his freedom to criticize established assumptions; or, rather, a series of orthodox interpretations have been imposed on works which seem, very conspicuously, to rebel against easy orthodoxies. For this reason, fairly detailed consideration is here given to the related social, historical, literary, and critical problems which arise in two works explicitly concerned with tyrannical authority: Chaucer's (deliberately) painful, poignant, and infuriating account of the 'needless' suffering endured by his gentle Griselda, and Webster's tragic portrayal of the cruel persecution suffered by his naturally virtuous, and always 'noble', Duchess of Malfi.

In some poems and plays, it is very difficult to decide which side to take, to determine who loses and who wins, who is victor, who victim. The third chapter, 'Of Their Vain Contest', is primarily devoted to the quarrel between Milton's Adam and Eve just after the Fall, where arguments and counter-arguments are so balanced that the result is a deadlock. There can be no end to argument, in such instances, since valid poetic and critical cases for one character and against his opponent can be countered by equally valid arguments against that character and in favour of his opponent.

Poetic deadlocks, in effect, leave the reader free to choose which characters and arguments he, personally, prefers. Yet how can one know whether one has chosen rightly? How can any critic be certain that his own responses to a work of art, his own imaginative insights into it, are perceptive and original, and not, in truth, far-fetched and perverse or altogether mistaken? How, in short, can the human imagination accurately evaluate its own reactions to the creations of another imagination—or even evaluate, accurately, its own products? The answer to this question may very well be, 'It can't'. At least it can never be absolutely certain that it *can*. Yet these questions are of great importance to criticism and poetry as well. So, for the purposes of discussion, the final chapters consider them in two different ways.

The fourth chapter, 'If This be Error', deals with characters, like Shakespeare's Troilus and Leontes, who face the consequences of mistaking their own imaginative convictions for empirical

realities; and with characters, like Hamlet, who find out for themselves whether the insights of their own imaginations are honest
ghosts or juggling fiends. In other plays considered here, Shakespeare and Marlowe explore the relationship between imagination
and truth to show how the individual may, in fact, freely become
what he imagines himself to be, but may finally become fatally
enthralled by his own imaginative conception of himself. 'Free
they must remain', the creators of certain characters imply, 'Till
they enthrall themselves'.

The final chapter, 'Stay, Illusion!', speculates about the powers
of poetry to deceive and enthral us, and, simultaneously, to set us
free with its truth. How far should the reader himself be taken in
by seductive poetry? If, for instance, one is totally carried away
by, say, Volpone's glittering, erotic fantasies, and consequently
decides, upon leaving the theatre, to act out all those fables of the
gods, or to imitate any number of Volpone's nefarious, yet
hilarious, tricks, then one would certainly have failed to notice
Jonson's obvious satirical criticism of all those fantasies, all those
tricks.[2] By contrast, if we are not taken in at all, if, like Jonson's
Surly, we refuse to be deceived, we will miss most of the fun, and
thus lose the rewards of poetry—including its luscious Dame
Pliants—to some Lovewit who can enter into the action, see the
truth, enjoy it, and license the show to go on. Indeed, in the
Epilogue to *The Alchemist*, the audience is cordially invited to
return and be taken in yet again by Jonson's poetry, including the
voluptuous fantasies of Sir Epicure Mammon and the tricks of the
many-faceted Face. Jonson even has the nerve to 'invite new
guests', who, like ourselves, and, indeed, like Mammon himself,
will hand over hard cash for the privilege of being deceived by
some player got up as Dol Common got up in the costume of the
Fairy Queen. To be totally deceived by 'the best of this kind',
which are but shadows, may be madness. Yet not to be deceived
at all seems madness too. It is like falling in love. To do so may
be to make a fool of oneself, to confuse reality and illusion, to lose
control; but the consequences of not doing so may involve an
even greater loss. When Mark Antony temporarily wishes he had
never seen and loved Shakespeare's own queen of the arts of love
and poetry alike, Enobarbus says,

[2] Yet one might, at that, have a rather spectacular time. Didn't Rochester, as
Alexander Bendo, copy Volpone, as Scoto of Mantua?

O, sir, you had then left unseen a wonderful piece of work; which not to have been blest withal would have discredited your travel.

And that's true, too.

My polemical attack on critics who have self-righteously refused to be 'blessed withal', and who, therefore, have rejected, and urged all of us to reject, some wonderful pieces of work, certainly does not deny their liberty, as individuals, to make whatever refusals they wish. It does, however, claim that the refusals and rejections in which they, themselves, take so much public pride have discredited their travels in the Alexandrias of poetry.

Contents

I Introduction: Poetic injustice: some winners and losers in medieval and renaissance literature

> . . . we'll talk with them too,
> Who loses and who wins; who's in, who's out;
> And take upon's the mystery of things,
> As if we were God's spies.
> *King Lear*

> You will draw both friend and foe, winner and loser.
> *Hamlet*

> As we went down the steps to the gravel I said,
> 'Prospero had a daughter.'
> 'Prospero had many things.' He turned a look on me.
> 'And not all young and beautiful, Mr. Urfe.'
> JOHN FOWLES, *The Magus*

A POET named Cinna just happens to wander out on the streets of Rome shortly after the assassination of Julius Caesar, and is dragged off to his death by a mindless mob. The young County Paris sets out to strew flowers on the grave of the beautiful woman he had hoped to marry, and dies as the result of his chance encounter with the desperate Romeo. Having risked the lives of twenty thousand men in a battle over a little patch of ground not even worth farming, Prince Fortinbras passes through Elsinore on his way home to Norway, and has the crown of Denmark offered to him.

Where is the justice in all this? Why does Shakespeare present us, on the one hand, with such seemingly gratuitous deaths, and, on the other hand, with such a gratuitous triumph? Why does he incorporate, within his great tragedy of the Roman state, the little tragedy of Cinna the poet? Why should his account of the 'misadventured, piteous overthrows' of Romeo and Juliet include the death of the 'good gentle youth', Paris? And why does Shakespeare force us to contemplate the golden fortune of a Fortinbras who fights over egg-shells, even as he confronts us with the untimely death of the brilliant and sensitive Prince of Denmark?

Neither the triumph of Fortinbras, nor the deaths of Cinna and Paris, are of any vital importance to the plots of the tragedies in which they occur. At least two major productions of *Hamlet*—the popular Olivier film, and the television version starring Nicol Williamson—cut out the entry of Fortinbras so as to focus all attention, in the end, upon the dead Hamlet. And the deaths of Paris and Cinna, deaths which might be considered 'but trifles' within the tragedies of *Romeo and Juliet* and *Julius Caesar*, could be cut without seriously altering the design of a larger action. Why, then, does Shakespeare devote dramatic time to the fates of minor characters who in no obvious way deserve what happens to them, who may die or triumph without even understanding why what has happened to them has happened to them?

And what of a major character, like De Flores in *The Changeling*, who does all sorts of vile deeds, yet wins exactly what he wants from life? De Flores wants only one thing. He wants to enjoy the beautiful Beatrice-Joanna. He does so—and, indeed, in the course of his play, he enjoys many things. When Beatrice summons him to perform a murder for her, he enjoys that:

> *Beatrice*. Come hither; nearer, man!
> *De Flores*. [*aside*] I'm up to the chin in heaven. (II. ii. 78–9)

He anticipates having her, and positively exults in that: 'the thought ravishes!'

> Methinks I feel her in mine arms already,
> Her wanton fingers combing out this beard,
> And being pleased, praising this bad face. (II. ii. 147–9)

Indeed, his single-minded desire gives De Flores a peculiar power, an extraordinary independence from other needs. He cannot be threatened, for, apart from having Beatrice, he rates his life 'at nothing'. He cannot be bribed, because he places wealth 'after the heels of pleasure', and thus can throw contempt on gold. Having become Beatrice's lover, he will commit any crime, from murder to arson, to assure their 'pleasure and continuance'. In the end, he takes pleasure in announcing to everyone that Beatrice belonged to him. He claims her even in death. 'Make haste, Joanna,' he commands: 'I would not go to leave thee far behind.'

A moralist might deem his death a just punishment for his foul deeds, but De Flores himself thinks only of the sweet reward those same misdeeds earned him in life:

> her honour's prize
> Was my reward; I thank life for nothing
> But that pleasure: it was so sweet to me
> That I have drunk up all, left none behind
> For any man to pledge me.   (v. iii. 167–71)

Everything that appals the other characters in the main plot of this tragedy gives satisfaction and pleasure to De Flores. However others may condemn his actions, De Flores exults in them. There is, in the end, no suggestion of sorrow, horror, or regret on his part. Those painful emotions are felt only by more virtuous characters. Yet again, where is the justice in all this?

In the course of this chapter, I shall argue that there is none at all. But before doing so perhaps I ought to supply a few reasons for here belabouring the obvious point that medieval and Elizabethan literature abounds with instances of 'poetic injustice' of various kinds.

Certainly most human beings need, and therefore profoundly desire, to see justice done. Yet this desire for justice is all too frequently frustrated in ordinary life, where discouraging examples of social and genetic injustice exist all around us. It is equally frustrating to turn to our history books and find in them a panorama of past events as bleak as the vision of future history which the Archangel Michael presented to Milton's Adam: 'So shall the World go on', says the Archangel, 'To good malignant, to bad men benign', until history and time alike shall cease—a view arrived at independently by Solzhenitsyn in *The First Circle*:

'History is so monotonous it makes you sick to read it. The more decent and honest a man is the worse he gets treated by his compatriots. The Roman consul Spurius Cassius Viscellinus wanted to give land to the common people, and the common people sent him to his death. Spurius Melius wanted to give bread to the hungry and he was executed because they said he was trying to get himself made Emperor . . . They put Gnaius Nevius in fetters to stop his writing plays in which he said what he thought. And the Aetolians proclaimed an amnesty to lure *emigrés* back and then put them to death. Even the Romans discovered it was more economical to feed a slave than to starve him, but that was afterwards forgotten. History is a farce from beginning to end. It's not even a matter of truth or error. There are no signposts to anywhere, and there's nowhere to go.'

In fact, the drama of human history has defied our best efforts to find laws of justice in it, and to impose rules of justice—or even of injustice—upon it. One of Solzhenitsyn's prisoners remembered

how Boris Sergeyevich Stechkin used to have to go and see Beria—in 1939 and 1940—*he* never came back empty-handed. Either the head of the prison would be sacked or we'd get more time for exercise. Stechkin could never stand all the bribery and corruption, and the difference in ration—eggs and cream for academicians, forty grams of butter for professors, and only half that much for the rest. He was a good man, Boris Sergeyevich—heaven help him—'
　　'Is he dead?'
　　'No, they let him out. And he got a Stalin Prize.'[1]

Neither the fetters of Gnaius Nevius nor the release of Stechkin can serve us as an example of some general law of historical justice or injustice. Nor can they provide us with instances of clear exceptions to some general rule. So far as historical justice and injustice are concerned, there appear to be no rules. And it is, perhaps, because the natural human desire for justice is so often frustrated by life and history that literary critics and common readers alike have, over the centuries, demanded that justice be done, at least in literature. At least, or so it has been repeatedly argued, we have the right to expect poetic justice from our *poets*. 'The good ended happily, and the bad unhappily,' says Wilde's Miss Prism; 'That is what Fiction means.' And far finer minds than hers have sought to find, in fiction, that ideal world located somewhere over the rainbow, where consequences correspond with actions, where 'moral orders' are always obeyed, where vice is punished and virtue rewarded.

Nevertheless, much of our greatest literature, precisely like the real world which it mirrors, persists in confronting us with certain characters who get a lot more, and with other characters who get a lot less, than they would have coming to them from any fair-minded judge or jury. For through their very fictions, poets like Shakespeare, Chaucer, and Webster insist upon bringing us right back down to 'this earthly world' where, in the words of Lady Macduff, 'to do harm' is often 'laudable', and 'to do good' some-

---

[1] *The First Circle*, trans. Michael Guybon (London, 1971), pp. 88, 84.

times accounted 'dangerous folly'; where, in the words of Cleopatra, 'some innocents scape not the thunderbolt'; where, in the words of Bosola, the only reward of doing well may well be only 'the doing of it'; where, in the words of Escalus, 'Some rise by sin, and some by virtue fall'; and where, in the words of the prisoner, Palamon,

> slayn is man right as another beest,
> And dwelleth eek in prison and arreest,
> And hath siknesse and greet adversitee,
> And ofte tymes giltelees, pardee.
>
> (*The Knight's Tale*, 1309–12)

So far as the great lords of medieval and Elizabethan poetry are concerned, it would seem that their duty to tell the truth about the human condition has very frequently taken precedence over even our most heartfelt public pleas for 'justice, justice, justice, justice'.

Thus, while it is obviously true that literature may sometimes give people just rewards for their misdeeds, it is also obvious that literature sometimes confronts us with suffering that cannot be conceived of as deserved. Indeed, the examples of justice and injustice provided for us in literature are as various, surprising, complicated, messy, and rich as those supplied us by life itself. For this reason, asking the question 'Do characters suffer or die because of their own flaws, sins or errors?' is finally, if ludicrously, comparable to asking the question 'Do gentlemen prefer blondes?', since the only true answer to either question necessarily has to be 'Some do, some don't'. And since those characters who do get just rewards for their misdeeds have always received their fair share of critical attention, it here seems, in all justice, right and proper to focus our attention, for a time, on some characters who do not get what they deserve, but simply get whatever their creator chooses to give them.

The winners and losers created by Chaucer, or by Shakespeare and his contemporaries, like the winners and losers created by the lotteries of genetics and evolution, differ radically in kind. Some characters, for instance, seem created to win and take all. These are the fortunate few who may win crowns, wealth, or beautiful women through no special merit of their own, but simply because they happen to be in the right place at the right time to take advantage of a situation which they have inherited, possibly without knowing of it in advance. Thus, all the whoring, cheating, scheming, acting, pimping, conniving, and gulling in *The Alchemist* ultimately serves to benefit Lovewit, who walks in at the end to claim all the spoils of the 'venter tripartite', and who gets the buxom, ripe, young, and rich Widow Pliant thrown in for good measure. And all the tragic suffering, scheming, cruelty, madness, and slaughter in *Hamlet* ends in the prophecy that 'the election lights/on Fortinbras'. 'My vantage doth invite me' to 'embrace my fortune', says the new heir apparent to the crown of Denmark; while the situation of all such walk-in winners is also summed up, by Shakespeare, in the following lines from *Cymbeline*:

> Many dream not to find, neither deserve,
> And yet are steep'd in favours; so am I,
> That have this golden chance and know not why.
>
> (v. iv. 130–2)

At the opposite pole from those characters who seem created to act the winning parts, there are literature's born losers. These are those characters who appear to have been created only in order to be ordered about, exploited, deceived, humiliated, or done in, without, in the process, enjoying a single moment of glory or even of individuality. One mark of such a character is that it is frequently difficult to remember his name—if, indeed, he has one. Joyce Cary once said that to preclude any active interest in, or sympathy for, certain characters, 'You take away their names.' And even when they have names, such characters are so undistinguished that it is frequently difficult to remember which was, say, Rosencrantz and which was Guildenstern. Should such undifferentiated types be so unfortunate as to come between the 'fell incensed points—Of mighty opposites' in a tragedy, the general reaction to the announcement of their deaths will be, as Tom Stoppard has reminded us, 'Who cares?' 'What of it?' 'So what?' If losers of this sort appear in a comedy, they are very likely to discover that 'all their harm is turned into a jape'.

Who, for instance, has ever felt seriously upset about the miserable lives and lamentable deaths of the Wife of Bath's first three husbands? Here is their own persecutor's gleeful account of a few of the many tribulations suffered by these 'guiltless' old men:

> O Lord! the peyne I dide hem and the wo,
> Ful giltelees, by Goddes sweete pyne!

For as an hors I koude byte and whyne.
I koude pleyne, and yit was in the gilt,
Or elles often tyme hadde I been spilt.

. . . .

They were ful glade to excuse hem blyve
Of thyng of which they nevere agilte hir lyve.

(*Wife of Bath's Prologue*, 384–92)

Receiving no compensation for their hardships, nor any sympathy from their audience, these nameless, faceless wretches endure deceit, false accusations, incessant nagging, endless harangues, the confiscation of their property, carnal overwork, and, possibly worst of all, occasional carnal deprivation, to go to their graves, remembered only as the three most henpecked husbands in the medieval world.

Few readers, if any, can have pondered the moral significance of the death of the second 'riotour' in *The Pardoner's Tale*. It is difficult even to remember him, for he is referred to only as 'that other'. Neither the youngest rioter, who decides to poison the others, nor the rioter who formulates the plot to kill the youngest one when he returns, this fellow seems to exist for the sole purpose of having the murder plan explained to him (and to us) in the most simplistic of terms.

That oon of hem spak thus unto that oother:
'Thow knowest wel thou art my sworen brother;
Thy profit wol I telle thee anon.
Thou woost wel that oure felawe is agon.
And heere is gold, and that ful greet plentee,
That shal departed been among us thre.
But nathelees, if I kan shape it so
That it departed were among us two,
Hadde I nat doon a freendes torn to thee?'
    That oother answered, 'I noot hou that may be.
He woot wel that the gold is with us tweye;
What shal we doon? What shal we to hym seye?'
    'Shal it be conseil?' seyde the firste shrewe,
'And I shal tellen in a wordes fewe
What we shal doon, and brynge it wel aboute.'
    '*I graunte,*' quod that oother, '*out of doute,*
That, by my trouthe, I wol thee nat biwreye.'
    'Now,' quod the firste, 'thou woost wel we be tweye,
And two of us shul strenger be than oon.

Looke whan that he is set, that right anoon
Arys as though thou woldest with hym pleye,
And I shal ryve hym thurgh the sydes tweye
Whil that thou strogelest with hym as in game,
And with thy daggere looke thou do the same;
And thanne shal al this gold departed be,
My deere freend, bitwixen me and thee. . . .'   (807–32)

Thus the first rioter gets the miserable second rioter to do most of the work. And given the intellectual capacity of a man who must be told, over and over again, that two are two, and one is only one, and that two are stronger than one, we may well wonder just how long he might have managed to keep his share of the gold. His pathetically few lines consist of a monosyllabic statement of a glaringly obvious fact; a monosyllabic statement of incomprehension; and several monosyllabic questions, concluding in an agreement to do what he is told. The two cleverer rioters outsmart each other, even as they underestimate each other, and the second rioter goes down in the process. In the Pardoner's exemplary tale, the fates of the first and third rioters may serve as superb examples of poetic justice—each has done unto him precisely what he had planned to do unto others. The stupid second rioter may be said to serve as an example of a 'stooge', or a 'fall guy' (American slang seems most appropriate here), whose final doom gets no more profound a reaction from us than does the humiliation of the cuckolded carpenter, John, within the comic context of *The Miller's Tale*.

This poor old man is tricked into performing a back-breaking day's work, and, while he is up in a tub sleeping off his exhaustion, his gorgeous young wife, his Alisoun, and her 'hende' Nicholas engage 'in bisynesse of myrthe and of solas' down in his very own bedchamber. At the fatal cry of 'Water!' he cuts the ropes, his tub falls down, he breaks his arm, and, as if that was not bad enough, 'the folk gan laughen at his fantasye'.[2] And so, of course, do we. This fact leads us into a critical and moral paradox. Instead of

---

[2] Unlike Carpenter John, the 'amorous Absolon' (another born loser if there ever was one) at least derives a lesson from his humiliation: 'Of paramours he sette nat a kers;/For he was heeled of his maladie.' The wretched carpenter is not nearly so lucky. He is in no way compensated for his hardships, either by the satisfaction of revenge or by any new knowledge. Instead, 'he was holde wood in al the toun'. My discussion of Chaucer's 'stooges' is based on a paper written by David Orgel, when he was a freshman student at Vassar College in 1971.

deploring the suffering involved in the fates of the Wife's first husbands, or of Carpenter John, one may actively relish their very woes, and thus join in the general laughter at them before dismissing them and their misfortunes with a shrug of indifference. Certainly most readers feel far less concern about these particular losers than they feel for significantly more villainous types, like Chaucer's Pardoner and Shakespeare's Shylock, who both win some sort of admiration or pity from their audience even as they are exposed or defeated by other characters.

By any standard of justice, we ought to reject Shylock and the Pardoner, and rejoice at their defeats in the same way we reject more innocuous losers. For surely the Pardoner is more dangerously evil, because he is so much more intelligent, than the second rioter he tells us about; while Shylock is a far more threatening and sinister figure within his comic context than was poor old John. The justice meted out to both Shylock and the Pardoner is poetic justice of the highest order. Yet many readers are not altogether pleased at their downfalls. 'As thou urgest justice', says Portia to Shylock,

> be assured
> Thou shalt have justice, more than thou desirest.
>
> (IV. i. 315–16)

And both Shylock and the Pardoner, or so it seems, are given more justice than some of us might desire, even as they are given precisely the defeats that they deserve. Here are some possible reasons why the just fates of the Pardoner and Shylock seem more disturbing than the unjust fates of other literary losers.

Both Shylock and the Pardoner are given great individuality. They are stunningly portrayed as outsiders in their literary worlds. Like a rare, custom-made, pistol with a hand-carved ebony handle, a character of this sort may evoke admiration and interest for reasons independent of the cruel function it is capable of performing—or rather, a recognition of its lethal purpose does not necessarily preclude an admiration for its unique and complex design. We are given detailed, close-up views of these characters and thus come to know them as we cannot know, say, the Wife of Bath's second husband. The Pardoner takes us into his confidence as he describes his nefarious confidence tricks, while the pain and suffering manifested by Shylock make the golden girls and lads surrounding him seem comparatively shallow and superficial. And, perhaps significantly, both these characters, at some point or another, are ridiculed or despised for something that they obviously could do nothing about—Shylock was born a Jew, and the Pardoner was impotent from birth. Indeed, Shakespeare calls attention to this particular form of literary genetics in his treatment of some of his other born losers, like Caliban and Cloten, who have been endowed by their own creator with brutish natures that they themselves cannot really help. These 'things of darkness', Shakespeare seems to say to us, 'I acknowledge mine'. Hence he sometimes gives them lines of great poetry and sometimes suggests that their bad behaviour (like Caliban's attempt to rape Miranda) was, while reprehensible, not—given the natures he has given them—unnatural. He also insists, from time to time, that we ourselves look at the world from their point of view. He thus lets us see beauty through the eyes of the beast, and view some of his winners through the very eyes of life's losers. He allows us to feel the force of Shylock's plea for common humanity, 'Hath not a Jew eyes?', even as he places that plea within its sinister context, and he repeatedly reminds us that Caliban was the original lord of Prospero's island. We are thus enabled, as if we were indeed 'God's spies', to understand, as well as to judge, such characters. And to understand is, in some measure at least, to forgive. The understanding of another person, the feeling of compassion for him, of sympathy with him, is, in art as in life, a kind of mystery, and Burke may have been right in asserting that 'where mystery begins, justice ends'.[3]

Furthermore, Shylock, Caliban, and the Pardoner are given wills and personalities all their own, so that, like individuals in real life, they are capable of surprising us—as the brute Caliban does when he describes the sounds of music that 'give delight and hurt not', or as the Pardoner does when he suddenly refers to Christ's true pardons. Our 'stooges', however, cannot so surprise us; for they are never permitted to break out of, or to transcend, the limited category or role in which they are fixed. Their personalities are defined and explained by the performance expected of them. Carpenter John thus exists, solely and specifically, as a type of the

---

[3] Quoted, entirely out of context, from *A Vindication of Natural Society*, in *The Works and Correspondence of Edmund Burke*, ed. F. Lawrence and W. King, vol. II (London, 1852), p. 548.

foolish old husband who did not heed the natural law whereby a man should wed after his 'simylitude' and who, therefore, 'moste endure, as other folk, his care'. We are told only what we need to know about such a character, and no more: the Wife of Bath's first three husbands were 'olde' and 'riche'. They were, quite obviously, produced, in triplicate, to fulfil a single literary function. Like very common, easily replaceable, mass-produced objects, they are treated—or, rather, mistreated and then discarded—in an identical way by Chaucer and Dame Alice alike. Thus they remain for ever classified together by number and status, and are described to us only in terms of the identical, and identically subordinate, parts which they played in the continuing saga of the Wife of Bath.

These, then, are some of the ways in which poets deliberately avert any serious involvement, on our part, with certain of their characters: they may define them solely in terms of some fixed category; they may take away their names and give them numbers; or they may make them carbon copies of each other, like Tweedledee and Tweedledum, Ambitioso and Supervacuo, or Bushy, Bagot, and Green. One reason why characters of this sort so frequently appear in duplicate or triplicate is surely that the more of them there are, the less of any one of them there is. Guildenstern, himself alone, might have had an individual identity which he simply cannot claim as the dramatic duplicate of Rosencrantz.

Yet apart from the obvious reasons supplied by their literary contexts, why should a master of characterization like Geoffrey Chaucer deliberately treat his own creations in such a manner? Why are so many of his characters so easily exploited by other characters, and so mercilessly exploited by Chaucer himself? In an absolutely desperate effort to moralize the existence of his 'stooges', one might argue that, through them, Chaucer may be teaching us some very pragmatic lessons. Human gullibility, he implies, may be either laughable or lethal. And if the gullible of the earth—a category which, alas, includes most of us—do not guard against our own gullibility, there will always be other rioters, clever clerks of Oxenford, and Wives of Bath around to take advantage of it.

In fact, characters who are intent upon taking advantage of, putting down, or keeping down, other characters may adopt methods markedly similar to those so successfully used by their creators to fix their lesser characters in some subordinate position. Iago, for instance, is the master of methods which strip other characters of their individuality. An expert at statistical reductions, Iago constantly locks his victims into closed compartments of age, sex, and race, classifying them in terms of their biological urges and sociological status. In Chaucer's *Clerk's Tale*, the Lord Walter treats Griselda as a writer might treat one of his minor characters. He behaves as if she were his own creation, confining her to the strictly limited role of an uncritically obedient wife, and evaluating her solely on the basis of her performance in that role. He insists, from the very outset, that she must never, by word or by deed, make manifest her individual thoughts and feelings. And indeed *The Clerk's Tale* effectively reminds us precisely what can happen when the reductive techniques so common in art are systematically used, by human beings in real life, to deprive other human beings of all their individuality and freedom. It becomes possible to perform experiments upon them; it becomes relatively easy to suppress any personal responses to their suffering. For that matter, the grim panorama of historical injustice includes millions of individuals whose names were taken away and replaced by numbers. It also includes countless people, like Cinna the poet, who have died simply because they happened to be in the wrong place at the wrong time.

Because the makers of history have themselves frequently been highly dramatic figures, or else have confronted highly dramatic situations, the classic historical drama, by its very nature, directs its primary attention to history's leading actors—to Caesar, to Brutus, to Richard II and Richard III. By contrast, the historical novel tends to focus our attention on comparatively ordinary people who are caught up in historical circumstances over which they have little, if any, control. *War and Peace*, for instance, is not 'about' Napoleon. 'If one were to think of *Lear* as a novel, then Edgar would probably have to be the hero'; or if the third part of *Henry VI* were turned into a novel, its hero might be the father who killed his son.[4] In *Julius Caesar*, it is through a helpless victim of history, through Cinna the Poet, that Shakespeare confronts us with that dimension of historical and social reality which, as Georg

---

[4] For full discussion, see Georg Lukács, *The Historical Novel* (London, 1969). Lukács quotes Otto Ludwig's remark about Edgar as hero of *King Lear* on p. 149.

Lukács has observed, is emphasized in the novel. For, though his main concern here is obviously with the fates of the great, Shakespeare does not forget, nor does he permit us to forget, how historical circumstances may affect the 'man in the street'.

Cinna the Poet differs from those who play the star parts in the tragedy of *Julius Caesar* in that he is given no choice whatsoever so far as his personal destiny is concerned. Brutus, for instance, chooses to participate in the conspiracy: he decides to let Antony address the mob; he even chooses his own death:

> Caesar, now be still:
> I kill'd not thee with half so good a will. (v. iv. 50–1)

By contrast, though Cinna himself has no will to do so, some chance, some fate, some 'something' prompts him to 'wander forth of doors'. He then encounters a mob of plebeians so intent upon violence that no answer to their questions can possibly satisfy them. Indeed, the dialogue between Cinna and his persecutors might have been written only yesterday, by Harold Pinter, so 'modern' seems its combination of absurdity and terror:

First Cit.	What is your name?
Second Cit.	Whither are you going?
Third Cit.	Where do you dwell?
Fourth Cit.	Are you a married man or a bachelor?
	. . . .
Third Cit.	Your name, sir, truly.
Cinna.	Truly, my name is Cinna.
First Cit.	Tear him to pieces; he's a conspirator.
Cinna.	I am Cinna the poet, I am Cinna the poet.
Fourth Cit.	Tear him for his bad verses, tear him for his bad verses.
Cinna.	I am not Cinna the conspirator.
Fourth Cit.	It is no matter, his name's Cinna . . .
Third Cit.	Tear him, tear him! (III. iii. 1–40)

Within the larger context of Shakespeare's tragedy of state, Cinna can stand for all victims of mob violence, for all helpless victims of external forces over which they have no control, which they do not understand, and to which they have contributed nothing. This is why the death of Cinna evokes its own special forms of pity and terror, and why it should not be cut; for though that death contributes nothing to the main plot of *Julius Caesar*, it contributes very significantly to the meaning and relevance of that tragedy.

Like political passions, personal passions may affect the destinies of others, and Shakespeare reminds us of that also. The
County Paris, in *Romeo and Juliet*, is treated coldly by Juliet and
run through by Romeo because of a love and marriage which he
himself knows nothing about. Given the point of view of Paris,
who had hoped to marry Juliet, her strange behaviour and un-
untimely death could only be interpreted in terms of her grief for
Tybalt. Taking flowers to Juliet's grave, the bereaved Paris is
enraged that anyone should interrupt his 'obsequies' and 'true
love's rite'. Then, when he identifies Romeo as the intruder, he
instantly assumes that the man who murdered his 'love's cousin'
must have come to the Capulet tomb to do some 'villainous shame'
to the dead bodies. None of Romeo's frantic lines urging him to
leave the tomb can make any sense to Paris, who has no way of
knowing the truth that lies behind those desperate pleas. Paris sees
Romeo only as he is outlined in the firelight of the feud, and therefore makes a fatal attempt to arrest the 'banish'd haughty Monta-
gue'.

It is Paris's behaviour towards him which finally forces Romeo,
against his will, to fight back. That behaviour was the result of an
essential misinterpretation of Romeo's motives and also of a failure
to realize that a crucial misunderstanding had taken place. Yet one
can only pity Paris, because it is so easy to understand why this
particular misunderstanding occurred. So many serious disagree-
ments result from misunderstandings, and from human failures to
identify and correct those misunderstandings, that almost anyone
who has had a fight with anyone else can sympathize with Paris
and Romeo alike. Given the emotionally charged situation, and
given the limited information concerning Romeo with which
Paris must needs interpret that situation, one can hardly blame
him for attempting to apprehend Romeo as a felon. Nor can we
specially blame Romeo for fighting back. After all, even in his
wild despair, Romeo tried his best to let 'good, gentle' Paris live.

Very much like Romeo in social status, in age, and in his grief
at the death of Juliet, Paris (again like Romeo) may be seen as a
tragic victim of a senseless feud which destroys willing participants, unwilling participants, and innocent bystanders without
regard to justice. Yet in contrast to Paris, Romeo is a tragic victor
as well: for what has been has been, and Romeo has had his Juliet,
while Paris is not only deprived of his life, but was also denied the

love he once thought he had won. In this, Paris is similar to Arcite, who loses love without ever having had it, in the end of Chaucer's *Knight's Tale*.

The fate of Arcite poses a peculiar series of problems so far as 'poetic injustice' and literary 'losers and winners' are concerned. It confronts us with the cosmic mysteries inherent in all those situations whereby, quite apart from any respective virtues and vices of our own,

> The bells of hell go ting-a-ling-a-ling
> For you, but not for me.

It also illustrates the injustice that must inevitably arise when two equally worthy candidates seek an identical goal which, obviously, only one of them may win.

Throughout *The Knight's Tale*, Chaucer insists that there is no earthly reason why Arcite specially deserved to lose life and love, or why Palamon specially deserved to live on 'in blisse, in richesse, and in heele'. He thus deprives us of the comforting assumptions that, after all, the best man will win, or, indeed, has won. For, all things being equal, there can be no 'best man'. And all things, so far as Palamon and Arcite are concerned, are shown to be as equal as things possibly can be. Or, to pose the problem in Marlowe's terms:

> When two are stripped, long ere the course begin,
> We wish that one should lose, the other win;
> And one especially do we affect,
> Of two gold ingots, like in each respect.
> The reason no man knows.   (*Hero and Leander*, 169–73)

Palamon and Arcite are as much alike as two gold ingots—indeed Chaucer alters the source of *The Knight's Tale* to make certain that they are, and so deliberately removes any reason why we ourselves should prefer one over the other.[5] They are the sons of sisters and

[5] Inquiring 'What was Chaucer's Aim in *The Knight's Tale*?'—*SP* 26 (1929), 375–85 —J. R. Hulbert points out that 'In the *Teseide* there is one hero, Arcita, who loves and is eventually loved by Emilia . . . Palemone is a secondary figure, necessary to the plot because he brings about the death of Arcita. The story is a tragedy, caused by the mistake of Arcita in praying to Mars rather than to Venus. In Chaucer's story there are two heroes, who are practically indistinguishable from each other, and a heroine, who is merely a name . . . In Chaucer's version . . . despite efforts of some scholars to show that there is a difference between Palamon and Arcite, it is hard to believe that anyone can sympathize particularly with either hero . . .' (p. 375). For fuller

sworn brothers. They are given equal time and sympathy by the
Knight; for instance, they suffer from separate, yet equal, misfortunes—the one in prison and the other in exile:

> Yow loveres axe I now this questioun:
> Who hath the worse, Arcite or Palamoun?
> That oon may seen his lady day by day,
> But in prison he moot dwelle alway;
> That oother wher hym liste may ride or go,
> But seen his lady shal he nevere mo.   (1347–52)

In their final tournament, their forces are so equally matched that
the spectators would be hard put to decide which side to bet on:

> For ther was noon so wys that koude seye
> That any hadde of oother avauntage
> Of worthynesse, ne of estaat, ne age,
> So evene were they chosen, for to gesse.   (2590–3)

They are also alike in the folly of their love for a distant princess,
who, for the greater part of the action, is not even aware of their
existence. 'This,' says Theseus,

> is yet the beste game of alle,
> That she for whom they han this jolitee
> . . . .
> She woot namoore of al this hoote fare,
> By God, than woot a cokkow or an hare!   (1806–10)

Thus, whereas the question 'who will get the girl?' is of para-
mount concern, a matter of life and death, to Palamon and Arcite,
the girl herself shows no preference for one knight over the other.
If she did, we might; but she does not. Emelye would prefer
chastity to marriage with either of the two noble kinsmen, but she
subsequently makes a virtue of necessity: first welcoming Arcite
as the winner, and finally marrying Palamon with bliss and melody.
The fair Emelye is surely one of literature's greatest nonentities.
Apparently designed solely to be the object of all desire, she is the
golden grail-girl in pursuit of whom the two knights sacrifice
years and years of time and are prepared to sacrifice their lives.
But the fact that she is so awfully, or so divinely, insipid, is surely

---

discussion of Chaucer's treatment of his sources, see *Sources and Analogues of Chaucer's
'Canterbury Tales'*, ed. W. F. Bryan and Germaine Dempster (Chicago, 1941); R. A.
Pratt, 'Chaucer's Use of the *Teseida*', *PMLA* 62 (1947), 598–621; and Elizabeth
Salter's very useful *Chaucer: 'The Knight's Tale' and 'The Clerk's Tale'* (London, 1969).

the result of a fine tragicomic irony of Chaucer's part. Speaking of Emelye, the Knight himself can only conclude that women follow fortune generally. So Emelye, the prize, will go to the one whom fortune favours, whichever one that might be.

Indeed, *The Knight's Tale* is crowded with references to 'fortune', 'aventure', and 'destinee' and to those unpredictable gods of love and war whose actions converge when Arcite dies, not as the result of any sin on his part, but as the result of a freakish accident. One moment before that accident, it was Arcite who rode in triumph to claim his love, while Palamon appeared to have lost. Everything could just as easily have gone the other way, and, for a brief moment, it did. Yet in the end, Palamon wins all and Arcite is dead. 'What is this world? what asketh men to have?' asks the unfortunate loser,

> Now with his love, now in his colde grave
> Allone, withouten any compaignye.   (2777–9)

From a larger perspective, Arcite is given a consolation prize in the end. He is, after all, for ever released from the 'foule prisoun of this lyf'. Thus, while death draws the line between the winner and the loser in *The Knight's Tale*, it is not considered a form of punishment for 'that goode Arcite'. Death, says the wise old Egeus, is simply the 'end of every worldly soore'. Nevertheless, one wonders if this statement would be of very much comfort to Arcite, who deemed his own particular death to be the end of every worldly *joy*: 'Allas, the deeth! allas, myn Emelye!/Allas, departynge of oure compaignye.' Arcite himself would naturally have preferred the fate of Palamon, whose subsequent life seems comparable to a fair palace rather than a foul prison, since he lives it out in health and wealth, with never a harsh word to disrupt the loving harmony which he enjoyed with his fair Emelye. Chaucer's final emphasis on the consolation of philosophy is of course not directed to Arcite, but to his own audience. It provides an alternative way of thinking about Arcite's death; it is mildly comforting, and thus releases Chaucer's characters and audience alike to celebrate with Palamon; moreover, it quite effectively prevents anyone from blaming Arcite for the early death sentence served upon him by the gods.

In the end of *The Knight's Tale*, we pity the loser and rejoice with the winner; and so we should have done had their titles been reversed. Because Chaucer deliberately presents his two knights to us as the literary equivalent of identical twins, we are prevented from becoming over-partial to either of his two gold ingots. Thus an alternative ending, with Arcite the winner and Palamon the loser, would be a mirror image of this one, and would evoke essentially the same emotional responses from us. In other works, however, Chaucer actively encourages his readers to take sides. We are invited to share the Wife of Bath's enjoyment of her triumphs over those first three husbands, and so to join with the winner in her laughter at the losers. By contrast, in *The Clerk's Tale*, Chaucer does everything he can to make his audience take the victim's side (see Chapter II). Thus, in art as in life, we sometimes may cheer the winner, while at other times we side with the underdog. At certain times it may be very difficult to decide which side to take, while at others we may become passionate partisans. And of course things become vastly more complicated when literary losers and winners with antithetical strengths and weaknesses, like, say, the golden King Richard II and the man of steel, Henry Bolingbroke, confront each other and each evoke conflicting responses from other characters and from their audience. In situations of this kind, critics may debate over which side we ought to take, and argue which side the author himself took; while at various points in a single reading, or in successive readings over a span of years, individual readers may shift their allegiances back and forth between the two characters, never quite certain whether they have chosen rightly (see Chapter III).

For us, as for the County Paris, the very act of perception entails interpretation, and so carries with it the danger of misinterpretation (see Chapter IV). We all interpret the motives and behaviour of other individuals—whether we meet them in literature or life—on the basis of whatever information about them happens to be available. For that matter, getting to know a person, as the psychiatrist Anthony Storr has observed, is often a matter of 'dispelling the smoke-screen of what we imagine he is like and replacing it with the reality of what he is actually like'.[6] The same is true of getting to know a work of art. Indeed, the fate of Paris can serve as a grim little allegory of criticism. Like individual responses to other people, responses to works of literature, and to the characters they contain, necessarily involve reception, selection, and in-

[6] *Observer*, 12 July 1970.

terpretation. Just as Romeo had motives beyond those assigned to him by Paris, a poem, play, or character has a reality of its own which is independent of, and may transcend, any interpretations, or misinterpretations, that are imposed upon it. This is why it is so important to test one's own interpretations, and those of others, against the work itself, and so remind ourselves of the limits of those interpretations. Otherwise, we, as critics, may find ourselves in a position comparable to that of Paris, who oversimplifies and misinterprets the evidence without even realizing that he has done so, and who therefore is subject to a lethal counter-attack.

Yet test them though we may, all our interpretations will necessarily remain subjective. For each individual brings to a work of art what he has experienced in life and in other works of art. He may then choose, from all the information supplied him by the artist, whatever he, personally, considers most significant. And the richer the context, or the richer the character, the more there is to choose from. The more a given character gives to his audience— in the way of passion, intelligence, entertainment, and so on—the more that audience will give him back in sympathy, understanding, fear, or admiration (Chapter V). From all that we discover about Hamlet, we each must select whatever seems most important to us, and finally base our interpretations of the character upon that selection. Various individuals may all observe the same action, all hear the same lines, and yet interpret them in entirely different ways. For instance, individual critics have interpreted Hamlet's hesitation to kill the kneeling Claudius as evidence of his sensitivity, of in inherent inability to make up his mind, of his determination to see Claudius damned, and of an Oedipus complex.

This process is especially obvious in the drama, when the director and actors have themselves chosen, from the many things they could have emphasized, those which they consider the most important features of a play or character, and so made their own selections and interpretations before presenting them to us. One actor, for instance, may make Shylock pitiable, another may make him despicable; one actor may make King Richard II seem a winner even as he loses, and another actor may make Boling-broke seem a loser even as he wins. But of course by the time a work of literature reaches us, or by the time a play reaches the producer, the author has already made the most crucial of all selections and interpretations. Chaucer could have told us a lot more about the Wife of Bath's first three husbands. For his own comic purposes he deliberately restricted our knowledge of them to their age, number, and economic status. And whereas we are given many impressions of Romeo—and thus know far more about him than Paris does—we know as little about Paris as Paris himself knew about Romeo. Moreover, certain characters, like people in real life, may change; so that the Richard II we see in the ending significantly differs from the Richard we met at the beginning of his tragedy.[7]

Certainly in many of Shakespeare's plays, and also in many of his greatest characters, all clear categories—including those of loser and winner, justice and injustice, joy and sorrow, right way and wrong way—are deliberately broken down. Characters may win great spiritual victories, yet lose material ones, and vice versa. For some characters, an excess of hubris or passion may be at once their greatest defect and their greatest asset, for, even if they live shorter lives, they live much more of life while they are living it. In tragedy, it is not necessarily death—which, after all, comes to everyone—but some experience of life, or some form of integrity of life, that draws the line between ultimate victory and defeat. For instance, characters who, secure within, feel certain that, under the circumstances, they did what was right, or simply did the best they could, may go down, as Eliot observed of Hamlet, 'fairly well pleased' with themselves.[8] They may, like the Duchess of Malfi, command their own executioners; they may, like Cleopatra and Brutus, even choose their own deaths. And certain young characters, who die far too early, can still say that they have 'answered well' and paid their score, that 'ere the first down bloomed on the chin', they sowed their fruits and got their harvests in. While they lived, they lived well. By contrast, Macbeth,

---

[7] Of course, 'whatever evolution this or that popular character has gone through between the book covers', his fate in the end remains fixed. 'No matter how many times we reopen "King Lear," never shall we find the good king banging his tankard in high revelry, all woes forgotten, at a jolly reunion with all three daughters and their lapdogs . . . similarly, we expect our friends to follow this or that . . . pattern we have fixed for them. Thus X will never compose the immortal music that would clash with the second-rate symphonies he has accustomed us to. Y will never commit murder. . . . Any deviation in the fates we have ordained would strike us as not only anomolous but unethical. We would prefer not to have known at all our neighbor, the retired hot-dog stand operator, if it turns out he has just produced the greatest book of poetry his age has seen.' Vladimir Nabokov, *Lolita* (New York, 1959), pp. 241-2.

[8] 'Shakespeare and the Stoicism of Seneca', *Selected Essays, 1917-1932* (London, 1932), p. 132.

who would wrongly win and played most foully in order to do so, finds that his desires—'King, Cawdor, Glamis, all'—were got without content, that all his battles won were battles lost. So he wishes he had died earlier, and in fact envies those he destroyed.

Certainly it seems obvious that how a tragic character ultimately feels about himself—how, looking back, he evaluates his life or confronts his death—is of crucial importance so far as the final impression left upon his audience is concerned. It thus is hard to see how, say, even a villain like De Flores, who knew what he wanted from life, won it, and found it precious enough to justify its cost, can be considered anything but a winner. That is, unless he is evaluated by standards other than his own. Yet scholars and critics, especially in the twentieth century, have frequently felt obliged to find fault with any given character's final evaluation of his own performance, and indeed to dispute the last judgement accorded him by his fellow characters and even by the author. A. L. French, for instance, finds it 'impossible to accept' Shakespeare's invitation 'to share Hamlet's view of Hamlet (which coincides with Horatio's and Fortinbras')'. By the end of the play, French complains, 'Hamlet is so deeply compromised that he ought not to be allowed to get off so lightly—get off, indeed, with a good deal of unction.' Shakespeare, according to the merciless French, has not meted out full justice to Hamlet: indeed, he has been 'indiscriminately lavish' in his generosity towards the dying prince.[9] Those flights of angels, in short, should have refused to sing Hamlet to his rest.

Adopting a posture of absolute critical objectivity, French informs us that he has reached his conclusions about *Hamlet* by 'standing back and pondering' the whole situation, and thus has overcome any 'alarming' tendencies to 'respond positively' to the 'sombrely elegaic cadences' of Horatio's farewell to his friend (p. 56). But in spite of his insistence upon his own objectivity, French's interpretation of Shakespeare's tragedy is just as subjective as that of anyone else. Like everybody else who has written about Hamlet, French has selected certain evidence from the information supplied him by the play, and has based his final interpretation of the character upon that selection. Indeed, it is inevitable that he should have done so; for the fact is that unprejudiced interpretation is mythical. In all sensation we pick and

---

[9] *Shakespeare and the Critics* (Cambridge, 1972), pp. 56–7.

choose, interpret, seek and impose order, devise and test theories about what we find:

'Why can't you draw what you see ?' is the immemorial cry of the teacher to the student looking down the microscope for the first time . . . The teacher has forgotten, and the student himself will soon forget, that what he sees conveys no information until he knows beforehand the kind of thing he is expected to see.[10]

A similar process occurs in literary criticism, and French provides a good illustration of it. After beginning his book by insisting how essential it is that 'we should make no assumptions of any sort about what we're going to discover' (*Shakespeare and the Critics*, p. 2), French then proceeds to contradict himself, apparently without realizing it, when he flatly assumes that we have all 'abandoned the romantic view of Tragedy, as represented and summed up by Bradley' and now 'see adverse criticism of the tragic hero as being an essential part of the tragic effect' in full accordance with the views of F. R. Leavis on *Othello* and L. C. Knights on *Hamlet* (p. 134). And of course, once having assumed that he would discover adverse criticism directed at Shakespeare's tragic heroes, French finds plenty of it. And so it always goes. Students encouraged to look for moral frailties in tragic heroes and heroines will find plenty of them, just as other students, looking for examples of heroic virtue, will find them in equal abundance. Those who set out in search of unifying themes or images will find their search rewarded with success. Whoever seeks Christ-figures will surely find Christ-figures.[11] And those who look for instances of poetic justice will find them as readily as those who look for instances of poetic injustice will find *them*. The point is not that this is wrong, but that it is inevitable. We each ransack the treasure troves of literature for what we personally (or even pro-

---

[10] P. B. Medawar, 'Hypothesis and Imagination', in *The Art of the Soluble* (London, 1967), p. 133.

[11] See Richard Levin, 'On Fluellen's Figures, Christ Figures, and James Figures', *PMLA* 89 (1974), 302–11. Inspired by Caliban, a friend and I once spent a pleasant hour thinking only of 'sympathetic monsters', and found enough of them, up to and including King Kong, to people a fairly weighty study of the type. Truly important critical breakthroughs, like Caroline Spurgeon's pioneering study of Shakespeare's imagery, occur when someone points out what was always there, always important, always true of the works involved, but had been generally overlooked by those who were themselves intent upon searching for something else. After Spurgeon, many others began looking for patterns of imagery.

fessionally) deem to be most valuable there. And what we find may, or may not, turn out to be of value to others.

It seems to me that the pursuit of objectivity has itself proved destructive to good criticism because it tends to require some form of authority apart from the individual texts themselves which can dictate how we all ought to think about those texts, or how we ought to respond to them. Critical definitions of what poetry and drama ought to be like, the conventions of the major genres, and the orthodox assumptions of a contemporary audience[12] all have, at one time or another, been invested with dictatorial power. So have individual critics. In an important discussion of F. R. Leavis, John Gross points out how *anyone* can confer a 'false objectivity' on his own preferences by dressing up a list of them, calling it a 'tradition', and so imply that they rest on 'stronger social and historical foundations than is actually the case'. Though 'Leavis has great things to his credit as a teacher—he woke his audiences up, he gave them a sense of direction—there is another side here, too. Good students welcomed him as an emancipator, and then found they had to spend years trying to escape from his liberating influence.'[13] For Leavis's theories became dogmas, and the mark of any dogma is that it is not subject to criticism by its adherents.[14]

[12] Scholarly books and articles in the 1950s and 1960s frequently implied that our own responses to a medieval or Elizabethan work should duplicate those of its original audience. If, say, 'the Elizabethans' would have damned the Duchess of Malfi for disobeying her brothers, then so should we. By this line of reasoning, if we could discover with certainty how the original audience felt, we would have objective evidence as to the proper interpretation of the work. But while we cannot know for certain about medieval or Elizabethan audiences, we do know how the original audiences responded to, say, Synge's *Playboy of the Western World* and to Ibsen's *A Doll's House*. And will it not be a travesty of criticism when some scholar, writing in the year 2500, conclusively proves (for instance) that by nineteenth-century standards, Torvald was an ideally indulgent husband; that the 'original audience' would have been rightly horrified when Nora slammed the door; and that, therefore, audiences in the twenty-sixth century should repress their 'modern' sympathy for Nora and side with Torvald too? For detailed criticism of the fallacies inherent in interpretations based on assumptions about original audiences, see Helen Gardner, *The Business of Criticism* (Oxford, 1959), Robert Ornstein, *The Moral Vision of Jacobean Tragedy* (Madison, Wis., 1960), William Empson, *Milton's God* (London, 1961), and Wilbur Sanders, *The Dramatist and the Received Idea* (Cambridge, 1968).

[13] John Gross, *The Rise and Fall of the Man of Letters* (London, 1969), pp. 279–80, 284.

[14] Of course creative writers themselves have always fought for freedom from such dogmas—see Doris Lessing's attack on critics like Leavis in her Preface to *The Golden Notebook* (London, 1972), p. 20—subsequent quotations are from the edition

However they may differ in other ways, unduly authoritarian schools of criticism have one thing in common. They all insist upon what they deem *ought* to be true of art, on what ought to go on in it. Any works which do not conform to the rules, or fit into the great tradition, or otherwise fail to do what they ought, may then be dislodged with remarkably little fuss. Alternatively, individual works may be reinterpreted in the light of the orthodox theory. Or the theory itself may prove to be so adjustable that almost any work may be shown to conform to it. For instance, according to the 'example theory' of comedy, the playwright should 'adorn his Images of *Vertue* so delightfully to affect people with . . . an emulation to practice it in themselves: and . . . render their Figures of *Vice* and *Folly* so ugly and detestable, to make People hate and despise them'.[15] The major weakness in this theory would at first glance appear to be its major strength. It is all-inclusive. The moral effect of any play whatsoever may be judged in the light of it. Over the years this theory has served as an easy weapon in the hands of moralists who have attacked the drama for violating it by creating villains and villainesses attractive enough to seduce the audience itself. On the other hand, defenders of the drama cite exactly the same theory to argue that the vices and follies exhibited on the stage were exposed rather than recommended. Thus, on the basis of precisely the same theory, the moral effect of precisely the same plays may be interpreted in diametrically opposite ways. A related theory, of course, is the theory whereby virtue, in literature, must be rewarded and vice punished. Once this theory takes hold of criticism, even characters that could serve to refute it can be forced to serve as illustrations of it. Thus clear instances of poetic injustice have been interpreted as examples of poetic justice (see Chapter II).

Yet the classic works themselves will continue to rebel against any tyrannical theory forced upon them, and thus may finally force

---

of 1962—and Randall Jarrell's classic attack on modern critical assumptions in 'The Age of Criticism' (reprinted in his *Poetry and the Age* (New York, 1953), pp. 70–95). It seems to me very disturbing that so many serious modern writers are actively hostile to literary scholarship and criticism—that is, if they are not bored stiff by it.

15 Shadwell, *Preface to the Humorists* (1671), quoted by Andrew Bear in his interesting discussion of the 'example theory', 'Restoration Comedy and the Provok'd Critic', in *Restoration Literature: Critical Approaches*, ed. Harold Love (London, 1972), p. 4.

a revision or rejection of the theory itself. For instance, the scholarly assumption that some moral or providential order ought to and, indeed, *must* have operated in the Christian literature of the Middle Ages and the Renaissance, cannot but run into resistance—into glaring distortions and difficulties—when it is imposed upon individual works such as *The Clerk's Tale* and *The Duchess of Malfi*, which themselves boldly dare to ask, with Chaucer's Palamon,

> What governance is in this prescience,
> That giltelees tormenteth innocence?

At some point in the future, it may, and I devoutly hope it will, seem a waste of time to argue the case for characters who are so obviously the innocent victims of cruel injustice as Webster's Duchess and Chaucer's Griselda. Yet here and now, at least, it seems legitimate to do so in order to raise some critical questions about authority in general, and to show how academic efforts to moralize, condone, or rationalize even the most conspicuous forms of poetic injustice have resulted in a critical failure to do justice to works which cannot but elicit outraged protests against some specific forms of social and political injustice.

II

'The victim's side': Webster's *Duchess of Malfi* and Chaucer's *Clerk's Tale*

> Why is it the gods do not feel indignation
> And come down in fury to end exploitation
> Defeat all defeat and forbid desperation
> Refusing to tolerate such toleration?
> > BRECHT, *The Good Woman of Setzuan*

> All I maintain is that on this earth there are pestilences and
> there are victims, and it's up to us, so far as possible, not
> to join forces with the pestilences.   CAMUS, *The Plague*

THOSE examples of poetic justice which do occur in medieval and
Elizabethan literature, and which seem so satisfying, have encouraged a whole school of twentieth-century scholars to find
other examples, and to force characters who do not yield to their
attempts into some moral framework whereby the injustices inflicted upon them are, somehow or other, justified. For instance,
our libraries are full of discussions of Elizabethan drama which 'go
so far as virtually to deny that any of the sufferers in a tragedy is
innocent', and which blame 'the errors and misdoings of major
and minor characters alike' for their tragic fates.[1] Any weakness
or peccadillo is enough to subject a character to critical cords and
whips. There are long essays about the misdemeanours of the
Duchess of Malfi and the indiscretions of Desdemona. To give
just one example of this critical method,[2] H. A. Mason deplores

the silence of the guilty pair [Othello and Desdemona] about their failure
to try the honourable means of getting married. It is damaging to both
—though much more damning against Desdemona—that they never
speak as if it had cost them anything to elope. It is a minor matter that
we get no light on the nature of the ceremony. What Christian priest or

[1] Helen Gardner, *Religion and Literature* (London, 1971), p. 27.
[2] I have discussed other examples in a different context, in *Likenesses of Truth in
Elizabethan and Restoration Drama* (Oxford, 1972).

▼

if not a priest what authority could make the marriage irrevocable?
. . . [With Desdemona] as with Juliet . . . we must allow for the
weight given by Shakespeare to the sin of disobedience to parents and
add to it our own uneasiness over the degree of deliberate deception
inevitably involved.[3]

And so it goes, on and on, in essay after essay, book after book.
Desdemona and Juliet disobey their fathers—off with their heads!
The Duchess of Malfi defies her brothers—off with hers. Yet
modern critics who rail against the 'sin' of 'disobedience' to
parents and other authorities conveniently overlook the obvious
fact that, in his comedies, Shakespeare gives such 'sins' no weight
whatsoever. To give only a few examples: Hermia and Celia both
disobey their fathers; Orlando disobeys his brother; Florizel
elopes with Perdita; and all of them live happily ever after, while
we ourselves feel not the slightest uneasiness over the 'degree of
deliberate deception inevitably involved'. And whatever happens
in comedy, so far as tragedy itself is concerned, it is, as Helen
Gardner has observed, 'an eccentric form of justice that metes out
the same punishment to errors and crimes alike and odd that it
should be thought consoling to conceive of the universe as ruled
by the Queen of Hearts' (*Religion and Literature*, p. 27). For that
matter, Matteo Bandello, the Renaissance writer who first wrote
down the story of the Duchess of Malfi, makes a powerful protest
against the *injustice* of the severe penalties imposed on women for
acts of disobedience which men could, and did, commit with vir-
tual impunity:

Would that we were not daily forced to hear that one man has murdered
his wife because he suspected her of infidelity; that another has killed
his daughter on account of a secret marriage; that a third has caused his
sister to be murdered because she would not marry as he wished! It is
great cruelty that we claim the right to do whatever we list and will not
suffer women to do the same. If they do anything which does not please
us there we are at once with cords and daggers and poison.[4]

In fact, poets like Shakespeare, Webster, and Chaucer can, if
they wish, enlist us on the side of their victims by confronting us
with cosmic and social injustices so cruel, so extreme, that we

---

[3] H. A. Mason, *Shakespeare's Tragedies of Love* (London, 1970), pp. 79–84.

[4] Bandello is quoted by Jacob Burckhardt in *The Civilization of the Renaissance in
Italy* (New York, 1958), p. 435. Though he elsewhere deplores the follies and frailties
of women, Bandello's points about the double standard still stand.

cannot but join in the protest against them. Certainly Webster, in his greatest tragedy, does everything he can to elicit our protests against the cruelties suffered by his heroine. 'The moral of this play, driven home as with the sledge-hammer of Dickens,' writes William Empson, 'is not that the Duchess was wanton but that her brothers were sinfully proud.'[5]

Certainly even a quick look at the text reveals which side Webster is on. His 'noble' Duchess of Malfi is radiant, intelligent, brave, witty, warm, and loving. In contrast to her brothers, she does nothing cruel or unnatural, nothing that would have subjected her to any serious criticism had she been a man: 'Why might not I marry?' she asks, 'I have not gone about in this to create— Any new world or custom.' In fact, throughout her tragedy, Webster insists that she acts in accordance with a finer and fairer morality than the one which persecutes and condemns her. Conversely, the tyranny of her brothers is consistently shown to be cruel, unnatural, and always unjust. Discussing the confiscation of the Duchess's property, one pilgrim asks 'by what justice' the dukedom was seized. The other answers, 'Sure, I think by none.' Then, finally appeased by her death, her brother Ferdinand acknowledges the outrageous injustice of his own behaviour towards her. What an 'excellent honest man mightest thou have been', he tells Bosola,

> If thou hadst borne her to some sanctuary!
> Or, bold in a good cause, oppos'd thyself
> With thy advanced sword above thy head,
> Between her innocence and my revenge!　(IV. ii. 275–8)

'What was the meanness of her match to me?' he goes on to ask,

> Was I her judge?
> Did any ceremonial form of law
> Doom her to not-being? did a complete jury
> Deliver her conviction up i'th' court?
> Where shalt thou find this judgement register'd
> Unless in hell?　(IV. ii. 299–304)

Bosola, likewise, proclaims the 'sacred innocence' of the dead heroine.

To argue that the Duchess deserved torture and death because

---

[5] William Empson, 'Mine Eyes Dazzle'—a review of Clifford Leech's *Webster: 'The Duchess of Malfi'*—reprinted in *John Webster*, ed. G. K. and S. K. Hunter (Harmondsworth, 1969), p. 297.

she chose to marry the man she loved and to bear his children is, in effect, to join forces with her tyrannical brothers. It is to preach what Empson calls an 'immoral morality' and to enter a world called 'historical' from which 'one's own conscience and knowledge of life are excluded'.[6] It is to condone a double standard of morality which today seems deplorable and which, even in its own day seemed conspicuously hypocritical and unfair.[7] It is, in short, to confuse the operation of some poetic justice of which we should approve with precisely those examples of social injustice which Webster does everything in his powers to make us condemn. Similarly, efforts to supply historical and theological rationalizations for Walter's persecutions of Griselda in *The Clerk's Tale* tend to turn Chaucer's fable upside-down, to deny its most obvious effect. Or so it will be argued here.

On a first reading, Chaucer's *Clerk's Tale* seems clear and simple in outline, characterization, and effect. A beautiful, helpless, compliant heroine suffers at the hands of her husband, whom she continues to love, with all her heart and soul, in spite of his cruel treatment of her. And the reader's own heart will be wrenched at Griselda's sad plight until the end, when he can rejoice with her as her losses are restored and sorrows end. The individual reader might also, along the way, either relish or find distasteful some of the more obviously sado-masochistic reverberations of the situation; or he might, in the words of a student of mine, find Griselda's patience 'damned irritating'. Nevertheless, our natural sympathies would clearly lie with Griselda, and we would, equally naturally, condemn Walter's irrationally cruel treatment of his wife. This, I believe, is a fair account of the obvious responses evoked by the tale.

Its position in *The Canterbury Tales* enriches *The Clerk's Tale* with some interesting complications. The Clerk tells the story of Griselda in response to the Wife of Bath, and thus places his tale within a larger dialectical context. The tale may have been explicitly intended to tease the Wife. Or it may represent a mild

---

[6] See *Milton's God*, pp. 95, 34. I disagree with many of Empson's conclusions about *Paradise Lost* but found his arguments highly relevant to *The Clerk's Tale* and *The Duchess of Malfi*.

[7] The unfairness of the double standard of sexual morality is pointed out by Adriana in *The Comedy of Errors* (ii. ii. 132–46) and by Emilia in *Othello* (iv. iii. 87–104). And see L. B. Wright, *Middle-Class Culture in Elizabethan England* (Chapel Hill, N.C., 1935), 465–507.

little clerk's preposterous dream of male domination, acted out by an incredibly demanding husband and an impossibly docile wife. For his tale enacts what may be a common masculine fantasy: have the beautiful, faithful, and perfectly obedient wife, yet remain free to get rid of her and her children, and replace her with a younger bride, without worrying about any claims or recriminations on her part. But, significantly, even as he presents this fantasy, Chaucer's Clerk criticizes it, almost as if the very imagination which had conceived of such a situation also, and simultaneously, condemned it as a fundamentally evil one. Furthermore, throughout the tale, the situation is presented, not in terms of the pleasure which it gives to Walter, but in terms of the pain it causes Griselda. Then, after having shown the potential suffering inherent in this particular fantasy should it be acted out in real life, the Clerk himself reminds his audience that, after all, the fantasy *was* only a fantasy; the tale was only a fiction. And of course the various husbands on the pilgrimage agree that ideally compliant women like Griselda seem to have vanished from the earth in the iron age of Dame Alice of Bath.

Of course this is only one of several possible accounts of the context. Obviously, none of these, or other perspectives provided by its position in *The Canterbury Tales*, can fully or finally explain why Chaucer deliberately emphasizes the human suffering implicit in the situation he inherited from Petrarch. Furthermore, quite apart from its affinities with fantasies, romances, and folk-tales, and apart from the comic 'Envoy' provided at the end, *The Clerk's Tale* appears to be an exemplary parable. Yet critical and scholarly efforts to explain precisely what it provides examples *of*, and to determine what the proper responses to those examples ought to be, themselves create serious problems for the modern reader.

Ideally, a full interpretation of a work written hundreds of years ago will reconcile historical, critical, and subjective interpretations of it in some fruitful and illuminating way, so that the work can be read on its own terms as well as (though not instead of) our own. For instance, a modern interpretation of *The Knight's Tale* might be based upon the critic's personal response to it, be influenced by twentieth-century ideas about some of the absurdities inherent in the ways of the world, and also be enhanced, supplemented, or corrected by pertinent information concerning the philosophy of Boethius, the conventions of medieval poetry, and the code of courtly love. It thus would be possible to interpret *The Knight's Tale* in terms of the literary, historical, and philosophical context in which it was written, and still read it, in Professor Leavis's words, 'as we read the living'.[8] But what happens if historical or theological interpretations of a comparable work do not complement but, rather, conflict with subjective responses to it? And, should various levels of scholarly interpretation contradict each other, which should finally take precedence over the others? Having taught Chaucer's version of the story of Griselda for some years now, it seems increasingly difficult to reconcile a modern and, admittedly, emotional response to its characters and situations with those theological and historical interpretations which, it has sometimes been argued, ought to govern any final responses to the tale.

If, for example, one considers Chaucer a staunch upholder of, and an uncritical apologist for, the medieval hierarchy, then the order of things in *The Clerk's Tale* must be seen to represent what is ultimately a right and proper one. The noble Marquis Walter wields absolute power over his subjects, who obey him in all things and, for the most part, accept even his most arbitrary decisions without question or criticism. Likewise, the man, Walter, holds total dominion over the woman, Griselda, who yields to his will in an ideally uncritical way—'ideally', since, according to medieval orthodoxy, and in the words of the tale itself,

> A wyf, as of hirself, nothing ne sholde
> Wille in effect, but as hir housbonde wolde.   (720–1)

Then, in the end, all turns out to be well. For, after all, the various powers exercised by Walter were supported by holy decree—'the powers that be' were said to have been ordained by God. And the tests which the Lord Walter imposed upon his wife are, finally, compared to the trials imposed upon the human soul by the Lord of Heaven. Thus the patient and obedient Griselda serves as an admirable example of how the human soul should endure adversity. Moralized in these terms, as it is by D. W. Robertson, Jr., *The Clerk's Tale* calls attention specifically to 'the duties of the Christian soul as it is tested by its Spouse', and it also 'systematically restores' the

---

[8] For an account of the way these issues arise in teaching, see the debate between Roma Gill and F. W. Bateson, 'As We Read the Living? An Argument', *Essays in Criticism*, 23 (April, 1973), 167–78.

proper matrimonial 'order' which was 'inverted' by the Wife of
Bath. If Robertson's interpretation is the right one, then further
discussion of the tale is effectively inhibited. So far as the twentieth-century reader is concerned, its power and significance are
diminished; its disturbing problems are easily solved; it becomes
a matter of historical interest only.[9]

Yet how can Robertson's interpretation be reconciled with the
primary responses elicited by the tale itself? And, given modern
standards, how can one be expected to accept, even temporarily,
theological and historical assumptions about the place of women
(or, for that matter, of subjects) in an 'order' that was once held
to be divinely sanctioned, but now seems simply the product of a
given set of cultural and social conditions? As Empson observes,
though we have recently 'heard much jeering at the idea of progress, it is clearly a moral help in dealing with ancient sacred
texts, which are always liable to give divine authority to some bar-
barous habit which was merely normal when they were written'
(*Milton's God*, pp. 198–9). And certainly our own experience with
rapidly changing social assumptions can help us to avoid the age-
old error of identifying the ideal with what is, or what was, merely
the *status quo*.

Thus, while it would obviously be mistakenly parochial to read
The Clerk's Tale from an exclusively modern point of view, it also
seems mistaken to read it solely in terms of the allegorical interpretation which is emphasized only at the end. For that interpretation tends to beg, rather than to answer, certain serious questions
about the exploitation and misuse of explicitly temporal powers
which are raised, on a very literal and human level, throughout the
tale itself.

Furthermore, while it obviously remains our responsibility
to find out as much as possible about the literary, historical, and
philosophical contexts in which a classic work was written, it is
also up to us, after doing so, to determine, in so far as we can, the

---

[9] Quotations are from D. W. Robertson, Jr., *A Preface to Chaucer: Studies in
Medieval Perspectives* (Princeton, N.J., 1962), p. 376. The counter-interpretation sug-
gested below was designed to open up speculation about the tale, though I realize
that my own discussion may be criticized, on the one hand, because it labours the
obvious; or, on the other hand, because it seems idiosyncratic, possibly altogether
wrong. Yet if this interpretation is, in fact, all too obvious, then it cannot be altogether wrong; and if it is entirely wrong, then it can hardly be the most obvious
interpretation.

individual author's intent in writing it; to ask whether the work itself upholds or challenges contemporary assumptions; and, finally, to decide for ourselves how we, personally, think and feel about it. If, say, new evidence turned up which conclusively proved that Chaucer, in this tale, was deliberately challenging certain assumptions on which the medieval hierarchy was based, then the tale itself would necessarily take on a set of meanings other than the orthodox ones assigned to it by Professor Robertson. In fact, for all we know, Chaucer might have set out, within the framework of the Petrarchan fable, to criticize certain contemporary orthodoxies.[10] For all we know: we cannot know for sure. We can only turn to the text itself. But while it would be dangerous to take it for granted that Chaucer critically questioned contemporary assumptions, it seems equally dangerous to take it for granted that he uncritically accepted them, that 'acquiescence, the act of conformity to whatever is traditional and established, was an essential . . . part of Chaucer's make-up', and that therefore we 'must . . . above all' avoid the temptation 'to place Chaucer "out of his age", as a revolutionary, a malcontent'.[11]

Why 'must'? Why 'above all'? Obviously no one is responsible for the norms which he finds to exist in society when he enters it, yet anyone as analytically intelligent as the mature Chaucer is surely capable of criticizing those social assumptions which he finds, upon reflection, that he is not prepared to support. For instance, one may counter interpretations of *The Clerk's Tale* whereby Chaucer condones tyranny in marriage, so long as the tyrant belongs to the right 'degree' or sex, with the argument that, throughout his works, Chaucer continually challenges, criticizes, and sometimes overtly attacks, the notion that any human being, of whatsoever sex, age, or 'degree', should have total power over another one.[12] And so far as theology is concerned, a number of

[10] Obviously, no artist can start from scratch, but he can criticize his forerunners. For full discussion, see E. H. Gombrich, *Art and Illusion* (London, 1968), and see also A. C. Spearing, *Criticism and Medieval Poetry* (London, 1972).

[11] Quotations are from Elizabeth Salter, *Chaucer: 'The Knight's Tale' and 'The Clerk's Tale*, p. 70.

[12] Furthermore, the notion of 'true gentilesse', so pervasive in Chaucer's works, was also subversive of the claims of social degree. See, for instance, *The Wife of Bath's Tale* (1150-8):

> For, God it woot, men may wel often fynde
> A lordes sone do shame and vileynye;
> And he that wole han pris of his gentrye,

basic tenets of Christianity itself were highly subversive of the
hierarchical powers so cruelly wielded by Walter. Apart from its
'golden rule', surely one thing all Christians might be assumed to
have been taught by the example of the founder of their religion
is that

> hye God somtyme senden kan
> His grace into a litel oxes stalle.   (206–7)

Indeed it can be argued that throughout this particular tale
Chaucer criticizes those social assumptions which enable Walter
to demand that Griselda render unto him the service due only to a
deity. For Griselda's situation is, from the very beginning,
described in explicitly social, economic, and political terms, as
well as in the obvious sexual and allegorical ones. And herein may
lie one source of the tale's peculiar power: it deals with forms of
tyranny, and of submission to tyrannical authority, which are not
only of great historical importance, but which still confront us,
here, now, in the second half of the twentieth century.

Thus it might be argued that whereas, from an allegorical point
of view—which gains support from the moral at the end of the
text, and from medieval theology and social theory as well—the
forms of tyranny portrayed in *The Clerk's Tale* are finally rational-
ized, from the dialectically opposite point of view—which may
also claim support from both the text and Christian doctrine—
they are criticized in a brilliantly subversive way. This second
interpretation would explain, as the allegorical interpretation does
not, why Chaucer consistently alters his sources, on the one hand,
to make Walter's behaviour towards Griselda so infuriating and
reprehensible, and, on the other hand, to make Griselda's uncritical acceptance of unnecessary suffering so very painful and
pitiable. It would also explain why Chaucer inserts the theological
interpretation of the situation which he inherited from Petrarch,
and which supplies his audience with an alternative frame of
reference, only after having criticized Walter more powerfully,

---

> For he was boren of a gentil hous,
> And hadde his eldres noble and vertuous,
> And nel hymselven do no gentil dedis,
> Ne folwen his gentil auncestre that deed is,
> He nys nat gentil, be he duc or erl;
> For vileyns synful dedes make a cherl.

frequently and severely than his predecessor.[13] Certainly, before he leaves us free to choose for ourselves between alternative literal and allegorical interpretations of the characters and situations, Chaucer deliberately encourages us to adopt a highly critical attitude towards the 'powers that be' as they manifest themselves in Griselda's Lord Walter.

'Taxation without representation is tyranny.' And until the very end of *The Clerk's Tale*, the gentle and virtuous Griselda is mercilessly taxed by tyrannical authority. Denied any control over her own fate, denied any voice in the decisions that most affect her life, Griselda suffers intolerable anguish, humiliation, and dread. Significantly, her supreme suffering has very little to do with Griselda as a unique individual, or even with her personal behaviour. Indeed, throughout this tale, Chaucer makes it glaringly evident that Griselda's suffering resulted from her having been born into social and sexual categories that made her vulnerable to tyranny, and from a tyrant's ruthless exploitation of her vulnerability.

When the noble Lord Walter proposes marriage to the humbly born Griselda, he makes the conditions of her future subjection clear enough:

> 'I seye this, be ye redy with good herte
> To al my lust, and that I frely may,
> As me best thynketh, do yow laughe or smerte,
> And nevere ye to grucche it, nyght ne day?
> And eek when I sey "ye," ne sey nat "nay,"
> Neither by word ne frownyng contenance?
> Swere this, and heere I swere oure alliance.'   (351–7)

Walter is to retain absolute freedom, absolute power, while Griselda is to renounce all freedom, all autonomy. She must never

---

[13] The theological interpretation comes, I think, too late to qualify effectively what was, and what remains, Chaucer's original emphasis on the literal human problems involved. For Chaucer's use of Petrarch, and of the French translation of the story of Griselda, see J. Burke Severs, *The Literary Relationships of Chaucer's 'Clerkes Tale'* (New Haven, 1942); W. F. Bryan and Germaine Dempster (ed.), *Sources and Analogues of Chaucer's 'Canterbury Tales'*; J. Sledd, '*The Clerk's Tale*: The Monsters and the Critics', *Modern Philology*, 51 (1953), 73–82; and B. H. Bronson, *In Search of Chaucer* (Toronto, 1967), pp. 104–7. Though Chaucer apparently did not know the *Decameron*, in his criticism of Walter he would seem to agree with Boccaccio, who concludes his version of the story of Griselda as follows: 'Can it not then be said here that even in the houses of the poor the divine spirits rain down from the heavens, whereas in royal houses there are those who are more worthy of watching over pigs than having rule over men?'

act independently of Walter's will. Whatever Walter may decide
to do to her, Griselda must not criticize him; she must never
express her own thoughts or feelings about his actions.

Griselda's social class is, of course, one source of Walter's
power over her. Himself secure in birth and wealth 'thurgh favour
of Fortune' (69), Walter continually reminds his wife that she is a
being of a lower order who owes everything she has, everything
she is in life, to him:

> 'Grisilde,' quod he, 'that day
> That I yow took out of youre povere array,
> And putte yow in estaat of heigh noblesse,—
> Ye have nat that forgeten, as I geese ?
>
> 'I seye, Grisilde, this present dignitee,
> In which that I have put yow, as I trowe,
> Maketh yow nat foryetful for to be
> That I yow took in povre estaat ful lowe,
> For any wele ye moot youreselven knowe.   (466–74)

Fixed, by birth, in an inferior category, and psychologically locked
into that category by Walter's attitude towards her, Griselda
always considers herself unworthy of her husband's favour:

> 'My lord,' quod she, 'I woot, and wiste alway,
> How that bitwixen youre magnificence
> And my poverte no wight kan ne may
> Maken comparison; it is no nay.
> I ne heeld me nevere digne in no manere
> To be youre wyf, no, ne youre chamberere.   (814–19)

Utterly convinced of her own unworthiness, and constantly reminded of it by Walter, Griselda never challenges his right to give
or to take away. Walter is her Lord. He is her Fortune. She is his
'thing':

> 'Ye been oure lord, dooth with youre owene thyng
> Right as yow list; axeth no reed at me.
> For as I lefte at hoom al my clothyng,
> When I first cam to yow, right so,' quod she,
> 'Lefte I my wyl and al my libertee . . .'   (652–6)

Griselda's humble birth also allows Walter to plead 'the tyrant's
plea', necessity, when he falsely claims that, because the people
resent her low origins, he must have her children done away with,
divorce her, and take a new, young, aristocratic bride:

> And though to me that ye be lief and deere,
> Unto my gentils ye be no thyng so.
> They seyn, to hem it is greet shame and wo
> For to be subgetz and been in servage
> To thee, that born art of a smal village. (479–83)

Thus Griselda's actual accomplishments as a governor—accomplishments admired by the very 'gentils' who Walter says resented her low birth—are dismissed. Here is the Clerk's account of the true public response to Griselda's performance as an administrator:

> Though that hire housbonde absent were anon,
> If gentil men or othere of hire contree
> Were wrothe, she wolde bryngen hem aton;
> So wise and rype wordes hadde she,
> And juggementz of so greet equitee,
> That she from hevene sent was, as men wende,
> Peple to save and every wrong t'amende. (435–41)

Yet Chaucer makes it clear that Walter can annihilate Griselda's personal accomplishments simply by waving the wand of class distinction over them. As both *The Clerk's Tale* and history remind us, regardless of whether a member of some despised social category excels at any job, any boss who wishes to get rid of such a person has traditionally been able to insist that 'the people' are complaining because they do not want to do business with, say, a Black, a Jew, a woman, or a kulak. The boss, of course, is extremely sorry about this; but, after all, he does have a duty to his clientele. 'Nat as I wolde, but as my peple leste' (490) is the way Walter puts it:

> My peple me constreyneth for to take
> Another wyf, and crien day by day;
> And eek the pope, rancour for to slake,
> Consenteth it, that dar I undertake;
> And trewely thus muche I wol yow seye,
> My newe wyf is comynge by the weye. (800–05)

Thus Walter passes the responsibility for his own free actions to the people beneath him and to the pope above him. And—so goes the line of tyranny—Walter's sergeant, in turn, passes the responsibility for *his* actions back to the Lord Walter:

> 'Madame,' he seyde, 'ye moote foryeve it me,
> Though I do thyng to which I am constreyned.

> Ye been so wys that ful wel knowe ye
> That lordes heestes mowe nat been ÿfeyned;
> They mowe wel been biwailled or compleyned,
> But men moote nede unto hire lust obeye,
> And so wol I; ther is namoore to seye.
>
> 'This child I am comanded for to take,'—   (526–33)

Walter's sergeant is just obeying orders.

Where can Griselda turn? She cannot ask Walter to disobey the will of his people, and she cannot ask the sergeant to disobey the will of his lord and hers. Griselda is trapped within a vicious circle of injustice and, worse still, she is forced to assent to that injustice. She must 'forgive' the sergeant. She must 'consent' to let him take her baby daughter away:

> Grisildis moot al suffre and al consente;
> And as a lamb she sitteth meke and stille,
> And leet this crueel sergeant doon his wille.   (537–9)

Now obviously there are times when we all, within reason, have to obey the orders of those in authority over us; indeed, Chaucer's Clerk reminded his audience of this fact before he began his tale:

> 'Hooste,' quod he, 'I am under youre yerde;
> Ye han of us as now the governance,
> And therfore wol I do yow obeisance,
> As fer as resoun axeth, hardily.   (22–5)

But when the subject of some absolute authority is required by that authority to act against his own reason, against his own convictions, against his own conscience, he can do only one of two things. He can, by his deeds, by his words, or at least by his thoughts, assert his own convictions: 'I am right and you are wrong. You have the power to do as you wish, but you will have to do it against my will.' Or he can choose to conform to the will of the authority. By an act of his own will he may make the will of the authority his own, and so behave in the way the authority wants him to behave. Meek, gentle, helpless, hapless Griselda thus conforms to her Lord's will:

> Allas! hir doghter that she loved so,
> She wende he wolde han slawen it right tho.
> But nathelees she neither weep ne syked,
> Conformynge hire to that the markys lyked.   (543–6)

Of course Griselda's humble obedience to his commandment that she give up her daughter does not satisfy Walter's irrational desire to test her for very long. He subsequently subjects her to other torments, for

> wedded men ne knowe no mesure,
> Whan that they fynde a pacient creature.   (622–3)

These lines do not appear in Chaucer's sources.

As A. C. Spearing has argued, the effect of this particular generalization, 'married men don't know when to stop when they find a wife who will put up with anything', is to 'relate the events of the story to our own experience of life, and to encourage us to judge them in the light of that experience, rather than to keep them in a separate compartment labelled "Literature Only"'.[14] Furthermore, the Clerk's sad generalization makes one wonder whether some show of resistance from Griselda might not have forestalled Walter's further persecutions. For, obviously, her perfect obedience in the first test does her no good at all. On the contrary: Walter's persecutions continue, step by slow step, as if he were trying to see how much degradation his wife can tolerate without fighting back. And so, given the way the story develops, Spearing concludes that 'what is surprising about it is not so much that Walter treats Grisilde as he does, as that, having started, he ever stops' (p. 97).[15]

At any rate, Chaucer apparently knew as well as any modern

[14] *Criticism and Medieval Poetry*, p. 83. In addition to works cited above, my discussion of *The Clerk's Tale* is indebted to, though frequently in disagreement with, J. Mitchell Morse, 'The Philosophy of the Clerk of Oxenford', *MLQ* 19 (1958), 3–20; Norman Lavers, 'Freud, *The Clerkes Tale*, and Literary Criticism', *College English*, 26 (1965), 180–7; and Alfred L. Kellogg, 'The Evolution of the "Clerk's Tale": A Study in Connotation', in his *Chaucer, Langland, Arthur; Essays in Middle English Literature* (New Brunswick, N.J., 1972), pp. 276–329.

[15] One thinks of the conversation between the heroine of Anne Brontë's *Tenant of Wildfell Hall* (Helen Huntingdon) and the dissolute Ralph Hattersley, who is married to a perfect Griselda—the good and virtuous Milicent:

'Is she not exactly the wife you wanted? [asks Mrs. Huntingdon] Did you not tell Mr. Huntingdon you must have one that would submit to anything without a murmur, and never blame you, whatever you did?'

'True, but we shouldn't always have what we want: it spoils the best of us, doesn't it? How can I help playing the deuce when I see it's all one to her whether I behave like a Christian or like a scoundrel such as nature made me? . . . [and] when she's so invitingly meek and mim—when she lies down like a spaniel at my feet and never so much as squeaks to tell me that's enough?' (*Novels of the Sisters Brontë*, ed. Temple Scott (Edinburgh, 1924), vol. II, p. 49.)

psychologist that giving 'a neurotic power-seeker all the power he wants does not make him less neurotic, nor is it possible to satiate his neurotic need for power. However much he is fed he still remains hungry.'[16] Indeed, Chaucer's readers are left to wonder whether, like Walter, they themselves might be capable of exploiting the vulnerability of those over whom they have too much power, and also to wonder whether, like Griselda, they might be capable of prostrating themselves before some tyrannical human deity. Certainly each of us in our lives plays many roles, and one man's Griselda may be another man's Wife of Bath, while one woman's adored Lord Walter may be another woman's miserable 'second husband'.

By dramatically showing the suffering inherent in the hateful doctrine that human beings should either dominate others or prostrate themselves, *The Clerk's Tale* may, in effect, leave the reader to wonder whether anyone really ought, ever, to be someone else's pebble or someone else's clod, and whether the question 'Who should rule?' (a question which demands an authoritarian answer) ought not to be replaced by the question 'How can we keep anyone from having too much power over others?' For Lord Acton's law about the corrupting nature of absolute power will swing into effect whoever rules; and, whatever class, sex, or race one may have been born into, whenever one begins to rule one becomes, by definition, a member of the ruling class.[17] And indeed, we have the 'Envoy' to *The Clerk's Tale* to remind us, if we need reminding, that wives, like subjects, who insist upon rights of their own, tend to get better treatment from their lords and masters than Griselda gets from Walter. For that matter, one lesson to be derived from *The Clerk's Tale* may be that in marriage, as in most human relationships, tyranny can only be avoided when all parties agree to observe the terms of a treaty that reads, in effect, 'You be good to me, and I'll be good to you'.

Griselda's marriage, as we have seen, was based on a very different kind of treaty: on a treaty which defined the husband, Walter, in terms of his absolute freedom, autonomy, and power, and which, therefore, creates the 'paradox of freedom' whereby any individual who claims *absolute* freedom can logically claim the

---

[16] A. H. Maslow, *Motivation and Personality* (New York, 1954), p. 346.
[17] See K. R. Popper, *Conjectures and Refutations: The Growth of Scientific Knowledge* (London, 1969), p. 345.

freedom to deprive others of all *their* liberty. Thus a marriage contract which maintains the unconditional freedom and power of a husband must necessarily define the wife, purely and simply, in terms of her unconditional surrender to his will. So the ultimate basis for Griselda's utter subjection to Walter is her contractual, social, and sexual status as his wife. In fact, Walter finally justifies his persecution of Griselda, and, in his own view, forestalls all criticism of it, with the following argument:

> 'And folk that ootherweys han seyd of me,
> I warne hem wel that I have doon this deede
> For no malice, ne for no crueltee,
> But for t'assaye in thee thy wommanheede . . .'

> (1072–5)

According to Walter, his tests of Griselda's womanhood—tests which seemed deliberately designed to outrage that very womanhood—involved no cruelty, no malice towards Griselda as an individual. Indeed, Chaucer makes it obvious that there was, after all, nothing *personal* in Walter's tests of his wife. The marquis always knew that Griselda was virtuous, patient, loving, obedient, and true. Certainly her behaviour, even by his own most exacting standards, proved exemplary throughout. Therefore she suffered all that pain simply because Walter wanted to perform experimental tests of her 'womanhood'.

There is, of course, an obvious reason why Griselda, who issued judgements of 'great equity' to others, never defies Walter. That reason is her love for him. *The Clerk's Tale* may, in fact, be read as yet another medieval 'allegory of love'—or, rather, it may be read as an allegory of tyrannic love in any age. For it is certainly true that many women who have found themselves physically, emotionally, economically, and socially dependent upon the man they adore have, like Griselda, had an opportunity to observe, at first hand, the operation of Lord Acton's dictum about power.[18] Here is Griselda's original version (it does not appear in the sources) of an old, old story:

> O goode God! how gentil and how kynde
> Ye semed by youre speche and youre visage
> The day that maked was our mariage!

---

[18] Of course men have also been victims of tyrannic love; but in comparison to women, they have generally been able to maintain a greater degree of social and economic autonomy.

> But sooth is seyd—algate I fynde it trewe,
> For in effect it preeved is on me—
> Love is noght oold as whan that it is newe.   (852–7)

'There are', says Simone de Beauvoir, 'few crimes that entail worse punishment than the generous fault of putting oneself entirely in another's hands.'[19] And de Beauvoir's description of the situation of the woman in love provides such an accurate gloss on Griselda's predicament that one need only apply it to Chaucer's heroine; the description itself need not be altered at all. Griselda provides a classic example of the 'loving woman whom man has not only revealed but created.' Her 'salvation' depends on the 'despotic free being that has made her and can instantly destroy her', and thus she 'lives in fear and trembling before this man who holds her destiny in his hands' (p. 400). Nevertheless, she will choose 'to desire her enslavement so ardently that it will seem to her the expression of her liberty'. Through 'her flesh, her feelings, her behaviour' she will enthrone her beloved as her supreme value and reality. 'She will humble herself to nothingness before him' (p. 375):

> Ther may no thyng, God so my soule save,
> Liken to yow that may displese me;
> Ne I desire no thyng for to have,
> Ne drede for to leese, save oonly yee.   (505–8)

> For wiste I that my deeth wolde do yow ese,
> Right gladly wolde I dyen, yow to plese.
>
> (664–5)

Griselda's love becomes her religion.

In what amounts to a total amalgamation of her will with his, and over and over again, Griselda prays that her Lord's will, not her will, be done on earth:

> She seyde, 'Lord, al lyth in youre plesaunce,
> My child and I, with hertely obeisaunce,
> Ben youres al, and ye mowe save or spille
> Youre owene thyng; werketh after youre wille. . . .'
>
> (501–04)

---

[19] *The Second Sex*, trans. H. M. Parshley (Harmondsworth, 1970), p. 399. Speaking of 'love' in *The Clerk's Tale*, one can speak only of Griselda. There is no evidence that Walter loved his wife, since he does everything possible to make her suffer, whereas loving a person means wishing to make him (or her) happy. This, by the way, was Thomas Aquinas' definition of love.

For Griselda, her beloved is the Lord whose name is blessed whether he gives or takes away.

All this is surely disturbing. Indeed, one could argue that, through the exaggerations of *The Clerk's Tale*, Chaucer is making his own 'modest proposal' about the potential suffering inherent in the assumption that one human being should have godlike power over another. For, after all, the relationship between Walter and Griselda simply carries to its logical conclusion the orthodox medieval assumption that a wife should have no will apart from that of her husband. And by any and all humane standards, whether pagan or Christian, medieval or modern, the Clerk's story of the relationship between Walter and Griselda is a horror story.

Indeed, the very first test that Walter puts her to requires Griselda to consent to an ultimate form of injustice; that is, to assent to the death of an innocent child. And of course when she is commanded by her living god to sacrifice her own child, Griselda behaves like Abraham.[20] In fact, the particular form of injustice embodied in such a command is so monstrous that the

---

[20] An excellent medieval gloss on Griselda's situation appears in the Brome *Abraham and Isaac* (see *Specimens of the Pre-Shakespearean Drama*, ed. John Matthews Manly (New York, 1967), pp. 41–57). 'Wel myghte a modder thanne han cryd "allas!"', writes Chaucer, as the sergeant takes Griselda's baby away; and Isaac tells Abraham,

> But, fader, I preye ʒow euer-more,
> Tell ʒe my moder no dell;
> Yffe sche wost yt, sche wold wepe full sore,
> For i-wysse, fader, sche lovyt me full wylle. (255–8)

Abraham, who loves his child as his life, yet will 'not spare for chyld nor wyffe,/But don after my Lordes lore' (81–5). 'A! Lord God', he prays,

> . . . my conseons ys stronly steryd,
> And ʒyt, my dere Lord, I am sore a-ferd
> To groche ony thyng a-ʒens ʒowr wyll. (78–80)

Writing about Stanley Milgrim's *Obedience to Authority* (London, 1974), Dachine Rainer argues that it may be imagination—the ability to feel the wounds of others as though they were your own—that results in the refusal to sacrifice others to some higher authority: 'One must be able to imagine what it is like to be wounded or deprived of life before one is prepared to refuse (despite *any* ideological persuasion) to inflict such injuries upon others' (*Sunday Times*, 2 June 1974, p. 12). It seems to me that the sympathetic imaginations of Chaucer and the anonymous author of *The Sacrifice of Isaac* must have compelled these writers to emphasize the inhumanity of ideological assumptions that parents should, upon demand, sacrifice their own children to the arbitrary will of some ultimate authority. Like Chaucer, the playwright stresses the human suffering inherent in the assumptions that lie behind his source story.

only assent possible, from any truly humane being, is some form of 'religious' assent. A striking modern literary analogue to Griselda's situation occurs when the priest, Father Paneloux, gives his assent to the suffering and death of an innocent child in Camus's *The Plague*:

[Paneloux] was not thinking of mere resignation or even of that harder virtue, humility. It involved humiliation, but a humiliation to which the person humiliated gave full assent. True, the agony of a child was humiliating to the heart and to the mind. But that was why we had to come to terms with it. And that, too, was why—and here Paneloux assured those present that it was not easy to say what he was about to say—since it was God's will, we, too, should will it. . . . 'My brothers,'—the preacher's tone showed he was nearing the conclusion of his sermon—'the love of God is a hard love. It demands total self-surrender, disdain of our human personality. And yet it alone can reconcile us to suffering and the deaths of children, it alone can justify them, since we cannot understand them, and we can only make God's will ours.'[21]

This sort of inhumane disdain of the 'human personality', this 'total self-surrender', this masochistic willing of one's own humiliation have, over long centuries, been considered praiseworthy forms of human virtue. Certainly an absolute, unquestioning obedience to the commandments of a superior authority has traditionally been praised in priests (and, for that matter, in soldiers) as well as in wives. In an essay about *The Clerk's Tale* and the theme of obedience, John McCall concludes that 'the whole tradition of obedience declares that the free submission of one's will to a human superior is the normal means by which one submits to the will of God' and that 'the essence of true obedience is to acquiesce in judgment as well as will—to make the desires of the superior one's own desires'. He also concludes that 'ideally, as with Griselda, the more irrational and irksome the command, the more ready and glad should be its acceptance':[22] 'Naught greveth

---

[21] *The Plague*, trans. Stuart Gilbert (Harmondsworth, 1972), pp. 184, 186.

[22] John McCall, '*The Clerk's Tale* and the Theme of Obedience', *MLQ* 27 (1966), 260–9. Given the tale, and the 'Envoy', McCall concludes that 'The alternatives are clear enough. One either sacrifices others to torment and death, or oneself—as Griselde did—to joy and life' (p. 269). I cannot see how these arguments make any sense at all in the context. McCall seems to believe that one must either dominate others or prostrate oneself, and that to prostrate oneself is better. But in submitting to Walter, Griselda was forced to 'sacrifice others'—her own children—ostensibly to death. An allegorical interpretation whereby (as in the epilogue to the Brome

me at al,' says Griselda to Walter, 'Though that my doughter and my sone be slayn,—At youre comandement' (647–9).

But is it really necessary to ask which attitude is more genuinely virtuous or, for that matter, more truly Christian: one that insists upon submission to an authority that inflicts suffering on human beings, or one that condemns such authorities in order to liberate men, women, and children alike from oppression? Evidently it is, in fact, necessary, time and time again, to ask ourselves, and to ask each other, which of these attitudes we really prefer. For the burden of freedom, of responsibility for one's own decisions and actions, will always be a heavy one, just as the thrill of submission to some all-powerful authority will always be a potent and addictive one. Thus both Chaucer and Camus confront their characters, Griselda and Paneloux, with what is essentially the same terrible choice: will they assent to, and, by giving their assent, condone, ultimate acts of injustice or will they deny the gods they love? Of course both Griselda and Paneloux, in obedience to their gods and for the love of their gods, assent to injustice. But we need not add our assent to theirs. Indeed, one need never uncritically accept the commandments of any authority —no matter how exalted—as the basis for one's individual moral judgements. For, after all, whatever authority we accept, we, as individuals, are the ones who choose to accept it. And, whatever authority gives us our orders, we are the ones who must decide whether it is right or wrong to obey them. Kant boldly carried these ideas into the field of religion, and concluded that, even if the Deity should reveal himself to us, we should still have to decide for ourselves whether or not to believe in him and worship him.[23]

Perhaps poor Griselda might have done better to decide not to believe in or to worship Walter. For, throughout his tale, Chaucer

---

Abraham and Isaac) children will be restored to their mothers, by the Lord, in some after-life, does not solve the moral problems which are posed, on a human level, in *The Clerk's Tale*.

[23] For full discussion, see Popper, *Conjectures and Refutations*, p. 26. Empson, following George Orwell, makes essentially the same point: 'Our own consciences are . . . the final judges even of truths vouchsafed to us by Revelation.' 'George Orwell very positively thought it the ultimate shame for a man to yield his conscience to an authority which craves to torture him and can only be restrained by a renunciation of thought, whether the authority is Stalin or God the Father' (*Milton's God*, pp. 257, 261).

deliberately departs from his own authorities, that is, his sources, in order to direct a series of devastating criticisms at Griselda's live idol. In line after line of passionate invective, the Clerk insists that Walter was no god at all, that he was not even a good human being:

> But as for me, I seye that yvele it sit
> To assaye a wyf whan that it is no nede,
> And putten hire in angwyssh and in drede.
>
> (460–2—*not in the sources*)

In Chaucer's version, Walter's plans concerning the fake papal bulls are motivated by his 'crueel purpos' (740), an expression not found in the Latin or French source; and later on, Petrarch's 'solito . . . ingenio' (v. i) is rendered as 'after his *wikke* usage' (785).[24] Furthermore, Chaucer alters his sources to insist that the suffering which Walter inflicted upon Griselda over all those years was needless, essentially absurd:

> What neded it
> Hire for to tempte, and alwey moore and moore . . .
>
> (457–8)
>
> O, nedelees was she tempted in assay! (621)

Given Chaucer's departures from his sources, it may be argued that in writing his *Clerk's Tale* he has acted in the cause of freedom of thought, of freedom to criticize established authority; that he has, in short, acted for the sake of precisely those freedoms that Walter denied to Griselda. Indeed, one could argue that he requires his own readers to exercise those freedoms in the reading of his story. For he constantly encourages us to speculate critically about the human problems which he so powerfully exhibits before us. One might also argue that, even as Camus incites his readers to rebel against the tyranny and injustice embodied in the plague, Chaucer deliberately incites his audience to protest against the forms of tyranny and injustice embodied in Griselda's less than divine marquis. Dr. Bernard Rieux, the narrator in *The Plague*, tells us that 'Summoned to give evidence regarding what was a sort of crime', and 'following the dictates of his heart', he has

---

[24] See Severs, *The Literary Relationships of Chaucer's 'Clerkes Tale'*, p. 231. I have used Severs's discussion of 'Chaucer's Originality' (pp. 229–38) and his texts of the sources throughout this chapter.

'deliberately taken the victims' side' (p. 246). Similarly, in *The Clerk's Tale*, the narrator takes the victim's side. Neither the Clerk nor his creator will permit us to argue that Griselda in any way deserved what happened to her, and there is no point even starting to argue that, because Griselda was persecuted, she really wanted to be persecuted, or that, because she submitted to her fate, she really liked it. There is a tyrant in *The Clerk's Tale*, and there is a victim, and Chaucer does everything he can to make certain that we do not join forces with the tyrant. Moreover, if the ways of man to woman in *The Clerk's Tale* are explicitly designed to be symbolic of the ways of God to man, then we remain free to criticize those ways as well.

Looked at from this angle, modern discussions of the tale which, in one way or another, attempt to explain away or even to moralize Walter's persecution of Griselda seem almost as disturbing as the tale itself. So do those which preclude us from critically examining its literary and historical problems from our own point of view.[25] Obviously any historical information that might illuminate Chaucer's poetry is to be welcomed. It is conspicuously true that Geoffrey Chaucer lived in a world which was quite different from our own, and we should try to learn as much as possible about that world. But one need hardly submit to authorities on the Middle Ages or, for that matter, to medieval authorities, in the same uncritical way that Griselda submitted to Walter. For instance, in the discussion of '*The Clerk's Tale* and the Theme of Obedience' cited earlier, John McCall himself would seem to have obediently submitted to the authorities on the subject of obedience, and uncritically accepted their arguments that 'the more irrational and irksome the command the more ready and glad should be its acceptance'.

[25] We need not even evaluate Chaucer's works in the same way that he himself may have finally evaluated them. If, for instance, one evaluates them by the standard of Chaucer's retractions, one might have to agree with B. H. Bronson (*In Search of Chaucer*, pp. 115–16) that the boring *Tale of Melibee* should be elevated over Chaucer's more 'earthly' writings, because it 'most completely answers the highest ends of mediaeval purpose'; it is 'most completely liberated from the impedimenta of mortality'; its characters, 'personifications duly named', are the 'most completely idealized'; and it is 'most packed with moral sentiment'. Thus it is a tale which 'Chaucer would never retract'. So far as those retractions are concerned, if I thought there was the remotest chance that I might writhe in an eternal bonfire as a result of some blasphemous remarks in this particular chapter, I would most certainly retract it and refer my readers to some less heretical essays. Wouldn't anyone?

But should it? In recent examinations of political tyranny, Bruno Bettelheim and John Passmore have argued that when we submit without question to authority, when we uncritically obey irrational orders, and when we physically or psychologically prostrate ourselves before our 'superiors', we voluntarily submit to the same dehumanizing mechanisms that the totalitarian state uses to impose its will upon its subjects. Writing about his own experience in Dachau and Buchenwald, Bettelheim concluded that the attitude of self-effacement adopted by many prisoners was an attitude which, 'more than any other, helped to produce the kind of childishly submissive, easily manipulated person the SS wanted'.[26] And the kind of person that the SS wanted (like the kind of wife that Walter wanted) was characterized by 'resignation, dependency, submission and passivity' (p. 149). Bettelheim goes on to observe that if the totalitarian state is also a class state, then it will wish 'to insure that each person will be fixed in his class as permanently as possible, so that he will not threaten the ruling elite by trying to advance in status'. Thus 'the SS would have liked to classify each prisoner for eternity' (p. 222), while Walter liked to keep Griselda constantly reminded of her base origins. Discussing the problem of tyrannical authority in a different context, John Passmore cites traditional arguments that the mystic must strip himself naked before he can be united with God, and then reminds us that the Nazis effectively used compulsory nakedness as a powerful weapon of humiliation.[27] Walter, of course, threatens Griselda with precisely this form of humiliation. And even as she maintains her status as a symbol of patience by echoing Job ('Naked out of my fadres hous . . . I cam, and naked moot I turne agayn'—871–2), Griselda manifests a profoundly human terror, and an explicitly sexual embarrassment, in what are some of the most painfully literal lines in *The Clerk's Tale*:

> Ye koude nat doon so dishonest a thyng,
> That thilke wombe in which youre children leye
> Sholde biforn the peple, in my walkyng,
> Be seyn al bare; wherfore I yow preye,
> Let me nat lyk a worm go by the weye.   (876–80)

The sheer nastiness of this particular situation demonstrates, on a

---

[26] Bruno Bettelheim, *The Informed Heart* (London, 1970), p. 191.
[27] John Passmore, *The Perfectibility of Man* (London, 1970), p. 314.

literal level, that whether or not the scourges of adversity sent to us by God may finally turn out to be for our own good, Walter's governance over her was never for Griselda's own good. Nor was his governance 'for the best' so far as Griselda's father, Janicula, was concerned. As a result of the cruel treatment of his daughter, Janicula cursed the day and time that nature shaped him to be a living creature (902–3—again, not in the sources).

It is true that even the most terrible scourges of adversity may, after all, prove of benefit to an individual: God 'preeveth folk al day, it is no drede',

> And suffreth us, as for oure excercise,
> With sharpe scourges of adversitee
> Ful ofte to be bete in sondry wise; . . .
> And for oure beste is al his governaunce. (1155–61)

Painful experiences can indeed prove 'for the best' if something important is learned from them. In this connection, several of the similarities and differences between *The Clerk's Tale* and *Gawain and the Green Knight* are illuminating. The Green Knight—as powerful within his poem as Walter in *The Clerk's Tale*—tests the virtuous Gawain, just as Walter tests his virtuous wife. And, like Griselda, Gawain does not know, at the time of certain tests, that he is in fact being tested. Thus, Gawain and Griselda are both surprised when the end of their tests is announced and their performance is assessed.

But Gawain learns something from his ordeals in the domain of the Green Knight. He returns to Arthur's court with a knowledge of himself and of the world that he did not have when he set forth. However painful his knowledge is to him, it is still knowledge; and, compared to the chastened Gawain, the courtiers who remained safe in Camelot seem like cardboard cut-outs. Furthermore, the poet encourages his readers to share Gawain's experiences with him, to feel that they themselves might have been seduced by the lady, or might have taken that magic girdle. We thus may share Gawain's painful new understanding of himself, as well as his astonishment at the Green Knight's revelations and final judgements. And like Gawain, many people, in real life, have had dangerous adventures that turned out to be miraculously instructive, if also humbling, tests of their moral integrity or their physical courage. But on other occasions, most people have had to live through episodes of needless, pointless, unnecessary suffering that teach them nothing whatsoever, yet must somehow be endured, somehow survived, before, at best, getting back to the place where they were when all the trouble began.

In the end, Chaucer makes it apparent that neither Walter nor Griselda learns anything from Walter's series of tests. Walter never even acknowledges, much less apologizes for, his infliction of pointless suffering upon an innocent person. Instead, the oppressor praises his obedient victim for passing unneccessary tests of her obedience, while the victim feels obliged to thank the 'benygne' tyrant for returning to her the children that he never should have taken away in the first place.

As opposed to his characters, Chaucer's readers may learn something from the tests, since they may examine them critically and reach their own conclusions about the final results. One might, for instance, conclude from the highly dubious reparations made to Griselda, who gets nothing back which was not wrongfully taken from her, that the exploited may remain exploited even when they believe they are receiving benefits from their exploiters. For even though she wins' back all she had thought lost, Griselda haunts the memory as one of literature's most pitiable losers.

The painful story of the patient Griselda brings to mind the parable of 'The Oxen' in Isak Dinesen's *Out of Africa*:

The oxen walk along within our own daily life, pulling hard all the time, creatures without a life, things made for our use. They have moist, limpid, violet eyes, soft muzzles, silky ears, they are patient and dull in all their ways; sometimes they look as if they were thinking about things.

There was in my time a law against bringing a waggon or cart on the roads without a brake . . . But the law was not kept; half the waggons and carts on the roads had no brakes to them . . . This made downhill work terribly hard on the oxen. They had to hold the loaded waggons up with their bodies, they laid their heads back under the labour until their horns touched the hump on their back; their sides went like a pair of bellows. . . . The oxen thought: 'Such is life, and the conditions of the world. They are hard, hard. It all has to be borne, —there is nothing for it. It is a terribly difficult thing to get the carts down the hill, it is a matter of life and death. It cannot be helped.'

If the fat Indians of Nairobi, who owned the carts, could have brought themselves to pay two Rupees and have the brakes put in order . . . then it could have been helped, and the oxen could have walked quietly down the hill. But the oxen did not know, and went on, day after day, in their heroic and desperate struggle, with the conditions of life.[28]

If Griselda is a heroine, her heroism is comparable to that of the oxen; it is the endurance of unnecessary, senseless, suffering. For Griselda, the loss of her children, her own sorrow and humiliation, all had to be borne. They could not be helped. But Chaucer himself insists that her suffering was 'needless', that it could have been helped. And while Griselda is described as a 'humble creature' who was disposed to endure the 'adversitee of Fortune' (756), we ourselves know that the slings and arrows of outrageous fortune which she had to suffer came, every one of them, from Walter himself. As Chaucer constantly reminds his readers, the responsibility for the suffering in *The Clerk's Tale* rests at the door of the human being who deliberately inflicted pain upon others. Yet this is an insight shared by Chaucer with his audience. It is withheld from Griselda herself. By contrast, Webster's Duchess of Malfi clearly recognizes the sources of her suffering, the injustice of her fate. She retains, quite independently of the other characters and, indeed, of the audience at her tragedy, the right to judge her oppressors. Thus, even though she loses everything—life, children, husband, all—the Duchess goes down a victor as well as a victim, as a tragic heroine whose integrity enables her to defy tyrannical oppression.

The Duchess does not 'account it praise to suffer tyranny'. From the very beginning, she insists on the freedom to criticize established assumptions, and so to reject intrusions upon her liberty to do what she, personally, considers right. Unlike poor Griselda, who was defined as a dutiful daughter, then as a dutiful wife, the mature Duchess has certain obvious advantages of birth and status which permit her to define herself; to behave in terms of her own conscience rather than submit to a conventional code of conduct imposed upon her by others. She is a widow, a comparatively independent woman, the governor of her own household, a great aristocrat, the very model of Castiglione's ideal court lady. In further contrast to Griselda, who was chosen by Walter, the Duchess does her own choosing. Like the Lord Walter himself, she claims the freedom to choose a partner in terms of virtue

---

[28] *Out of Africa* (New York, 1970), pp. 263-4.

rather than rank. So great is her individual integrity, her aristocratic pride, that whatever happens to her, however others defame her, she can proclaim herself 'Duchess of Malfi still'.

Indeed, her superb contempt for her persecutors is comparable to that of certain 'upper-upper class' prisoners whose behaviour in the concentration camps so profoundly impressed Bettelheim. The formerly 'anointed' prisoners 'seemed to develop such a feeling of superiority' that nothing done to them in the camps could damage them psychologically: 'How well they stood up was quite remarkable'. For they retained 'the last freedom' that not even the concentration camp could take away—the psychological and intellectual freedom to decide for themselves how to think and feel about the conditions of life. And if we can exercise that freedom, Bettelheim concludes, 'then if we cannot live, at least we die as men'.[29] 'Whether I am doom'd to live or die,' says the Duchess, 'I can do both like a prince' (III. ii. 70–1).

Whereas comedy tends to commend conformity, tragedy frequently glorifies rebellion, resistance, freedom, independence, and individuality. It is her brave resistance to tyranny that gives the Duchess a tragic stature which, however pathetic her predicament, Griselda cannot and does not claim. The noble Duchess gives 'majesty to adversity'; even her melancholy seems to be 'fortified' with 'a strange disdain'. These descriptions of her behaviour come from her persecutors, just before Ferdinand is driven mad by the sight of her dead body, and Bosola is inspired by her heroism to take up the sword of justice and avenge her death. Like submission to tyranny, resistance seems to be contagious, and so Bosola, who began, like Walter's sergeant, by simply obeying orders, is converted to the cause of the Duchess. The example of her 'integrity of life' thus extends beyond her death to the end of the play.

The differences between *The Clerk's Tale* and *The Duchess of Malfi* suggest alternative methods that poets may use to elicit an audience's protests against injustice. By presenting his readers with

---

[29] *The Informed Heart*, pp. 173, 240. See also p. 147: 'Those prisoners who blocked out neither heart nor reason, neither feelings nor perception, but kept informed of their inner attitudes even when they could hardly ever afford to act on them, those prisoners . . . came to realize what they had not perceived before; that they still retained the last, if not the greatest of human freedoms: to choose their own attitude in any given circumstance.' Prisoners who 'understood this fully, came to know that this, and only this, formed the crucial difference between retaining one's humanity' and forfeiting it to the SS.

a meek, gentle, passive, victim who cannot criticize, much less rebel against, her all-powerful persecutor, Chaucer—by way of his Clerk—incites his audience to espouse the cause of Griselda against Walter's oppression. Webster has his heroine so heroically lead the resistance to tyranny that she may inspire members of the audience, even as she inspires Bosola, to join forces with her against the cruelty, injustice, and hypocritical morality of her brothers.

Taken together, these works imply that, in real life, the only way to behave towards a tyrannical authority which refuses to accept any rational criticism is to resist it. As *The Duchess of Malfi* reminds us, a tyrant may destroy any individual who dares to defy his power; yet sustained resistance may finally overthrow the tyrant. If the Duchess, because she dies, can be considered defeated by her tyrannical brothers, they, in turn, are ultimately defeated by her influence. Moreover, the Duchess dies well, on her knees only before God, while her brothers go down howling: Ferdinand on all fours; the Cardinal on his knees—before Bosola. Like the domain of the great Calabrian Duke Ferdinand, the domain of the Lord Walter is a realm of unreason. Neither tyrant heeds criticism of any kind. Walter acts out his most wildly irrational whims, and Griselda uncritically yields to his most perverse demands. Nothing whatsoever is done to correct an insane situation until Walter miraculously comes to his senses and stops the tests. In the absence of rational criticism, in the absence of any resistance from Griselda or anyone else, nothing short of a miracle could have stopped Walter's cruel experiments from continuing. In Webster's tragedy, the emotionally healthy and natural Duchess is tortured and killed by the combined power of Church and State, as embodied in the heartless Cardinal and the unnatural, obsessive, and bestial Ferdinand. Yet though she is surrounded by madmen, she herself does not go mad:

> I'll tell thee a miracle—
> I am not mad yet, to my cause of sorrow.
> Th' heaven o'er my head seems made of molten brass,
> The earth of flaming sulphur, yet I am not mad.
>
> (IV. ii. 23–6)

Always capable of withstanding the madness of the society that persecutes her, constantly asking the great critical questions, 'Why?' and 'Why not?', the Duchess seems a dazzling star illuminating a dark world, and her star shines still, even now, three centuries after the first production of her tragedy.

Thus Chaucer and Webster attack injustice, defend their helpless victims, and prosecute their own persecutors. Their readers serve them as a court of appeal that remains free to rule, as the evidence requires—and as common humanity requires—in favour of the innocent and injured parties. For 'after all the refinements of subtlety and the dogmatism of learning', it is by the common sense (and sensibility) of readers who are uncorrupted with scholarly prejudices that the characters and situations in medieval and Elizabethan literature, like those in any other literature, must finally be judged.

In the next works to be discussed here, the process of doing justice to characters of different kinds becomes more complicated, since the cases for and against an individual character, or characters placed in opposition to each other, are so equally balanced that the result may be a series of literary and critical deadlocks.

III

'Of their vain contest': Poetic and critical deadlocks in *Paradise Lost* and Spenser's bower of bliss

> Sore hath been thir fight,
> As likeliest was, when two such Foes met arm'd;
> For to themselves I left them, and thou know'st,
> Equal in their Creation they were form'd . . .
> Whence in perpetual fight they needs must last
> Endless, and no solution will be found.
> God's account of the war in heaven.

> In necessary things, unity: in doubtful things, liberty; in all things, charity.   RICHARD BAXTER

WHEN they wake up after the Fall, Milton's Adam and Eve are, at first, confounded, stricken mute, unable or unwilling to say anything to each other. Then mistrust, suspicion, anger, and hatred lead each to blame the other for actions which led to their loss of innocence and love. Adam blames Eve for having insisted upon going out to work in the garden alone:

> Would thou hadst hark'n'd to my words, and stay'd
> With me, as I besought thee, when that strange
> Desire of wand'ring this unhappy Morn,
> I know not whence possess'd thee; we had then
> Remain'd still happy, not as now, despoil'd
> Of all our good, sham'd, naked, miserable.   (IX. 1134–9)

Eve then blames Adam for permitting her to leave his side:

> Being as I am, why didst not thou the Head
> Command me absolutely not to go,
> Going into such danger as thou said'st?
> Too facile then thou didst not much gainsay,
> Nay, didst permit, approve, and fair dismiss.
> Hadst thou been firm and fixt in thy dissent,

Neither had I transgress'd nor thou with mee.

(IX. 1155–61)

'Thus they in mutual accusation' spent the 'fruitless hours', and 'of thir vain contést appear'd no end' (IX. 1187–9).

Given the sequence of individual decisions and actions that led to the Fall, Adam and Eve could indeed go on debating 'who was most to blame' for the rest of their lives. Neither of them could ever win this particular debate; but, then, neither could finally lose it. There are valid and invalid arguments on both sides, and so long as, 'neither self-condemning', each continues to blame the other, Adam and Eve will remain trapped in a logical, psychological, and emotional deadlock. For Milton himself makes it clear that they were both to blame, but that they were guilty in dialectically opposite ways. Their argument is thus comparable to a lawsuit where cases for and against the plaintiff and defendant are equally good and equally flawed. And, of course, Milton's readers who have been witnesses to the crime, may themselves become active participants in the contest.

One might certainly agree with Adam that Eve was to blame for being too adventurous: she should not have gone out looking for temptation (IX. 364–9). Or we might agree with Eve that Adam was at fault: he should never have let her go into danger alone. Someone else, however, might argue that she was right to go, that 'our bold mother' acted for the sake of human independence and freedom by rejecting a fugitive and cloistered virtue. And, for that matter, perhaps Adam should have let her do as she wished, since 'force upon free Will hath here no place' (IX. 1174), and 'what', after all, 'is Faith, Love, Virtue unassay'd?' Raphael has explained why God refused to impose force upon Adam's will—

> good he made thee, but to persevere
> He left it in thy power, ordain'd thy will
> By nature free, not over-rul'd by Fate
> Inextricable, or strict necessity;
> Our voluntary service he requires,
> Not our necessitated, such with him
> Finds no acceptance, nor can find, for how
> Can hearts, not free, be tri'd whether they serve
> Willing or no, who will but what they must
> By Destiny, and can no other choose?   (V. 525–34)

—so why should Adam forcibly impose his will upon Eve's?

Certainly Milton himself refuses to interfere with the freedom of his readers to reach their own conclusions about the characters and situations in *Paradise Lost*. He evades no issues, shirks no difficulties, and so has presented arguments and counter-arguments for and against his God, his Satan, his Adam, and his Eve. Thus the individual reader remains free to decide which of the characters and arguments he, personally, prefers.

And so, over the centuries, poets, scholars, and critics alike have become passionate partisans for and against God, Satan, Adam, Eve, *Paradise Lost*, and Milton himself.[1] In fact, Milton presents so many situations, arguments, and characters from diametrically opposed points of view that critics, in whatever hereafter is assigned to them, may very well go on arguing about the individual cases for all eternity. And at different times in life, the same reader may himself see and interpret the epic characters and their actions from entirely different angles. Perhaps a quick look at Milton's handling of the relationship between Adam and Eve can illustrate the power and glory of his method of characterization and argument, even as it illustrates some of the problems this method poses.

The poet's goal may sometimes be, as Ben Jonson said, 'to make the spectators understanders'. And, while the decision whether to approve of or to condemn them is left to us, one object of Milton's poem is surely to make us understand his Adam, his Eve.

When we first see them, hand in hand in their garden, they are described as complementary, but not equal, beings:

> both
> Not equal, as thir sex not equal seem'd;
> For contemplation hee and valor form'd,
> For softness shee and sweet attractive Grace,
> Hee for God only, shee for God in him.   (IV. 295–9)

Of course it is Eve who occupies the inferior category, and, significantly, she knows she does. Whereas Adam had his time

---

[1] For useful accounts of critical responses to Milton, see *Milton: The Critical Heritage*, ed. John T. Shawcross (London, 1972); *Milton: Modern Judgements*, ed. Alan Rudrum (London, 1968); R. M. Adams, *Ikon: John Milton and the Modern Critics* (Ithaca, N.Y., 1955); A. J. A. Waldock, *'Paradise Lost' and its Critics* (Cambridge, 1947); *The Living Milton*, ed. Frank Kermode (London, 1960); and *Milton: Modern Essays in Criticism*, ed. Arthur E. Barker (New York, 1965).

alone on earth, Eve found him there, with all his sovereign claims
upon her, from the time of her creation. Having first admired her
own image in the water, Eve has subsequently been instructed
that, however lovely, her image is inherently inferior.[2] 'There I
had fixt/Mine eyes till now', she tells Adam,

> Had not a voice thus warn'd me, What thou seest,
> What there thou seest fair Creature is thyself,
> With thee it came and goes: but follow me,
> And I will bring thee where no shadow stays
> Thy coming, and thy soft imbraces, hee
> Whose image thou art, him thou shalt enjoy
> Inseparably thine, to him shalt bear
> Multitudes like thyself, and thence be call'd
> Mother of human Race: what could I do,
> But follow straight, invisibly thus led?
> Till I espi'd thee, fair indeed and tall,
> Under a Platan, yet methought less fair,
> Less winning soft, less amiably mild,
> Than that smooth wat'ry image.   (IV. 465–80)

Her first response is to turn away from Adam; but he claims her as
his own, as one for whose creation he was responsible, and who
therefore belongs to him:

> back I turn'd,
> Thou following cri'd'st aloud, Return fair *Eve*,
> Whom fli'st thou? Whom thou fli'st, of him thou art,
> His flesh, his bone; to give thee being I lent
> Out of my side to thee, nearest my heart
> Substantial Life; to have thee by my side
> Henceforth an individual solace dear;
> Part of my Soul I seek thee, and thee claim
> My other half.   (IV. 480–8)

With that, his gentle hand seized hers; she yielded, and 'from that
time' has acknowledged,

> How beauty is excell'd by manly grace
> And wisdom, which alone is truly fair.   (IV. 490–1)

---

[2] See Cleanth Brooks, 'Eve's Awakening', reprinted in Rudrum, *Milton: Modern
Judgements*, pp. 173–88, for the theory that Eve recapitulates the process of a child's
growing up and thus transferring the affections to the other sex. Brooks points out
that, in Freudian terms, the case of the female child is specially difficult, since it must,
in transcending the mother image with which it has first associated warmth, nourish-
ment, and affection, transcend an image of its *own* sex.

Her sole claim to superiority over Adam—her beauty—is thus, from the outset, rendered insignificant in comparison to Adam's wisdom.

Yet Eve realizes that her inferior status affords her certain advantages. From one point of view, she enjoys 'the happier Lot', having a consort 'Preëminent by so much odds'—for surely most human beings enjoy knowing superiors from whom they can learn. Conversely, Adam's superior position itself has its liabilities: 'like consort' to himself, he can 'nowhere find', and so lacks the companionship of a true equal (IV. 446–8). Milton thus presents a hierarchy in which all created beings have certain advantages and disadvantages. His God oversees a rationally ordered hierarchy wherein those above have been invested with specific virtues and qualities which justify their comparatively exalted status in the order of things. Therefore, so long as the assets and liabilities of one's own position, and the inherent superiority of those above, are freely and lovingly recognized and accepted, all will be well.

Yet Milton also implies that the tendency to rebel against even the most benevolent establishment is somehow inherent in the very nature of free beings; that there is a kind of second law of universal dynamics whereby the force which imposes stability and order will always be countered by an opposing force of equal energy, if not of equal power. And first through Satan, then through Eve, Milton suggests that some subordinate, whether in heaven or on earth, will inevitably ask *why* he (or she) should have been for ever relegated to an inferior status.

So far as their dialectical relationship on earth is concerned, Adam tends to be the spokesman for the established order, while Eve asks critical questions about it.[3] Adam's superior reason provides the proper answers to her questions; yet in raising them, Eve demonstrates her own capacity for independent thought and intellectual initiative. Indeed, by the time of her fatal encounter with Satan, Eve's desire to rise above her subordinate position and her wish for some knowledge of her own that would free her from childlike dependency upon Adam seem quite as natural as her original willingness to accept her lot.

For this particular Eve has been endowed by the poet who created her with qualities other than the soft, attractive graces.

[3] Adam, in turn, asks questions of Raphael. Yet in their discussions with each other, Eve seems the most curious, the most critical. She is the one who asks 'why?'.

She also exhibits the 'masculine' capacities for contemplation and for valour. It is her bold initiative that leads the way to the fall, and her contemplative analysis of the tragic situation afterwards which shows the way back towards reconciliation. Eve is also the one who, on earth, echoes Satan's great question, 'why should it be sin to know?'.

> One fatal Tree there stands of Knowledge call'd,
> Forbidden them to taste: Knowledge forbidd'n?
> Suspicious, reasonless. Why should thir Lord
> Envy them that? can it be sin to know,
> Can it be death? and do they only stand
> By Ignorance, is that thir happy state,
> The proof of thir obedience and thir faith?   (IV. 514–20)

In her demonically inspired dream, these questions are implanted in Eve's mind, and so is the desire to rise to a state of higher wisdom, to glimpse a perspective larger than the limited one allotted her. Like Marlowe's Faustus, she dreams of flying up to the clouds, of rising above and looking down upon 'the Earth outstrecht immense', a prospect 'wide' and 'various' (v. 86–9). The absence of Adam from Eve's dream of freedom is conspicuous, and so significant. Before this, Adam's image was with Eve even in her dreams. Indeed, her dream may indicate a need, a wish to escape from Adam's pervasive presence which subsequently manifests itself in her suggestion that they work independently for a while. For however wise and loving an authority may be—and Adam has the combined authority of a father, a husband, and an overlord, it is frustrating always to be told what one should think, or how one should behave.

Throughout the debate that precedes the fall, Eve asks questions that reflect her desire for some autonomy, her determination to prove herself Adam's equal in *something*. She considers his unwillingness to let her go an insult to her integrity, and tells him he ought to consider her his equal, at least in that:

> If this be our condition, thus to dwell
> In narrow circuit strait'n'd by a Foe,
> Subtle or violent, we not endu'd
> Single with like defense, wherever met,
> How are we happy, still in fear of harm?
> But harm precedes not sin: only our Foe
> Tempting affronts us with his foul esteem

Of our integrity . . .

. . . .
And what is Faith, Love, Virtue unassay'd
Alone, without exterior help sustain'd?
Let us not then suspect our happy State
Left so imperfet by the Maker wise,
As not secure to single or combin'd.   (IX. 322–39)

Adam gives the right reason why she should stay with him in spite of all her arguments. Then he yields to them:

But if thou think, trial unsought may find
Us both securer than thus warn'd thou seem'st,
Go; for thy stay, not free, absents thee more.   (IX. 370–2)

By now determined to prove herself in deed as well as in dialectic, Eve acknowledges the validity of his final argument, but first she carefully makes his permission official:

With thy permission then, and thus forewarn'd
Chiefly by what thine own last reasoning words
Touch'd only, that our trial, when least sought,
May find us both perhaps far less prepar'd,
The willinger I go, nor much expect
A Foe so proud will first the weaker seek;
So bent, the more shall shame him his repulse.
Thus saying, from her Husband's hand her hand
Soft she withdrew.   (IX. 378–86)

So, having won her first real argument with the lord of the earth, Eve leaves him, tragically overconfident of her powers to contend with the Lord of Hell.

At the time of her fall, Eve does not succumb to Satan's flattery (IX. 615–16); rather, she responds to his claims that the 'intellectual fruit' will supply what she knows was denied her at creation: that higher wisdom 'which alone is truly fair'. In the fatal moment of decision, Eve's aspirations are primarily intellectual:

In plain then, what forbids he but to know,
Forbids us good, forbids us to be wise?

. . . .
What fear I then, rather what know to fear
Under this ignorance of Good and Evil,
Of God or Death, of Law or Penalty?
Here grows the Cure of all, this Fruit Divine,

> Fair to the Eye, inviting to the Taste,
> Of virtue to make wise: what hinders then
> To reach, and feed at once both Body and Mind?
>   So saying, her rash hand in evil hour
> Forth reaching to the Fruit, she pluck'd, she eat.
>   (IX. 758–81)

In her desire to achieve wisdom and power for herself, Eve forgets all about Adam. Though she later tells him that she took the fruit for his sake, the truth is that Adam entered her mind only after she had first tasted the fruit of Knowledge for herself alone:

> But to *Adam* in what sort
> Shall I appear? Shall I to him make known
> As yet my change, and give him to partake
> Full happiness with mee, or rather not,
> But keep the odds of Knowledge in my power
> Without Copartner? so to add what wants
> In Female Sex, the more to draw his Love,
> And render me more equal, and perhaps,
> A thing not undesirable, sometime
> Superior: for inferior who is free?   (IX. 816–25)

Who indeed? And why should one be explicitly forbidden to remedy that inferiority if it is possible to do so? Eve takes the fruit in order to escape from a static and limited role, to exert some influence over her own destiny, to transcend her biological condition, and to remedy her ignorance. She thus acts, from one point of view at least, in accordance with those uniquely human ambitions which, over the millennia since she ate that fruit, have been the source of human dignity and greatness. And, given her situation, who would not have done the same? The point is that Milton enables us to understand and, in doing so, to sympathize with Eve's desire for knowledge which would make her autonomous, fully equal, and perhaps, sometimes, superior; to feel upon our pulses the excuses for her failure in obedience and love.

At the time of her fall, Eve thinks only of herself. At the time he tastes the fruit, Adam thinks only of Eve. In his great imaginative re-creation of the Fall of man, Milton suggests that, because human beings inevitably take for granted whatever they have in abundance, they will risk the loss of any paradise they may already possess in order to gain that which they do not have, or to hold what they cannot take for granted. It is because she was so certain of Adam's love that Eve could seek independence from it, and dream of freedom from his authority. Indeed, she takes Adam's love for granted to such a degree that, when she decides to offer him the fruit, it never occurs to her that he might refuse it:

> Confirm'd then I resolve,
> *Adam* shall share with me in bliss or woe.　(IX. 830–1)

And of course her confidence proves justified; for Adam has never been able to take Eve for granted. From the time he first glimpsed her in a dream he has feared, above all else, that he might lose her:

> The Rib he form'd and fashion'd with his hands;
> Under his forming hands a Creature grew,
> Manlike, but different sex, so lovely fair,
> That what seem'd fair in all the World, seem'd now
> Mean, or in her summ'd up, in her contain'd
> And in her looks, which from that time infus'd
> Sweetness into my heart, unfelt before,
> And into all things from her Air inspir'd
> The spirit of love and amorous delight.
> Shee disappear'd, and left me dark, I wak'd
> To find her, or for ever to deplore
> Her loss, and other pleasures all abjure.　(VIII. 469–80)

Created first, as lord of the world, Adam has already experienced autonomy. But he has also experienced loneliness, found it intolerable, and asked God for a companion. Thus, while Eve strives for independence from him, Adam wants complete union with her. He lets her go into danger alone because he fears that forcing her to stay might result in an emotional alienation between them more profound than any physical separation—that her stay, 'not free', would 'absent' her more. He will take the fruit because he cannot endure the thought of life alone again, without her:

> How can I live without thee, how forgo
> Thy sweet Converse and Love so dearly join'd,
> To live again in these wild Woods forlorn?　(IX. 908–10)

For Adam, he and Eve 'are one'. To lose her would be to lose part of himself (IX. 958–9). He thus will have no other Eve after her:

> Should God create another *Eve*, and I
> Another Rib afford, yet loss of thee
> Would never from my heart; no no, I feel

> The Link of Nature draw me: Flesh of Flesh,
> Bone of my Bone thou art, and from thy State
> Mine never shall be parted, bliss or woe.   (IX. 911–16)

And he will have no other God before her: his duty to God is quite as conspicuously absent from his mind, when he takes the fruit, as her duty to him was absent from her mind when she first touched and ate.

Whereas Eve fell because she aspired to superiority, Adam fails both himself and Eve when he endows her with the consummate perfection, the absolute self-sufficiency of a deity:

> when I approach
> Her loveliness, so absolute she seems
> And in herself complete, so well to know
> Her own, that what she wills to do or say,
> Seems wisest, virtuousest, discreetest, best;
> All higher knowledge in her presence falls
> Degraded, Wisdom in discourse with her
> Loses discount'nanc't, and like folly shows;
> Authority and Reason on her wait,
> As one intended first, not after made
> Occasionally; and to consummate all,
> Greatness of mind and nobleness thir seat
> Build in her loveliest, and create an awe
> About her, as a guard Angelic plac't.   (VIII. 546–59)

While Eve always sees when Adam is 'least wise' (VIII. 578), his uncritical adoration of her beauty leads him to fail to protect her as he might have done. His passion blinds him to the facts that she needs him just as much as he needs her and that the perfection which he attributes to her is possessed only by God. It also leads him to sin against the image and glory of that God which was in himself. 'Was shee thy God?' asks his Judge,

> that her thou didst obey
> Before his voice, or was shee made thy guide,
> Superior, or but equal, that to her
> Thou didst resign thy Manhood, and the Place
> Wherein God set thee above her made of thee,
> And for thee, whose perfection far excell'd
> Hers in all real dignity: Adorn'd
> She was indeed, and lovely to attract
> Thy Love, not thy Subjection.   (X. 145–53)

The exclusively self-centred life may lead us, like Eve, to fail others. Yet it also seems wrong to depend upon some other fallible human being for all our happiness, nor should we deny the divine voice within for the sake of some live idol without:

> Oft-times nothing profits more
> Than self-esteem, grounded on just and right.
>
> (VIII. 571–2)

Adam's situation, as governor, required the highest rational and critical knowledge of himself and Eve, even as it required the highest love. His problem is comparable to that of a parent who cannot bear to risk, even for its own good, the affection of a beloved child, and who places an unfair burden on that child by depending on its success, by making it the sole source of his happiness. One may thus sympathize with Adam's situation as profoundly as one may sympathize with Eve's. For if most people have experienced the problems of the governed, they also, at different times, may have to face the problems of the governor. Ideally, of course, one should avoid centring *everything* upon either one's self or another individual, and thus fulfil both oneself and one's obligations rightly. Love Eve without deifying her; love Adam without worrying about being superior or inferior to him. That is the ideal, but how difficult it is for human beings to achieve is made evident in the situation between Adam and Eve in *Paradise Lost*—that situation which poses the problems faced by both husband and wife, lover and mistress, parent and child, governor and governed.

Returning now to their 'vain contest', it becomes even easier to argue that Eve was too adventurous, or that Adam was too uxorious. Where Eve behaved in a bold, aggressive way in sallying forth to meet a great adversary, 'domestic' Adam behaved in a soft and yielding way, adopting the traditionally 'feminine' position of the one who stays behind, waits, and wreaths a garland for the returning conqueror. Yet perhaps more illuminating than any of these arguments is the recognition that the attributes of both sexes, in *Paradise Lost*, as in life, are shown to reside in both— contrasting with each other, yet coexisting within the individual. And what is true of the 'two great sexes', the masculine and feminine principles which 'animate the world', is also true of good and evil:

Good and evil we know in the field of this world grow up together almost inseparably; and the knowledge of good is so involved and interwoven with the knowledge of evil, and in so many cunning resemblances hardly to be discerned, that those confused seeds which were imposed on Psyche as an incessant labor to cull out and sort asunder, were not more intermixed. It was from out the rind of one apple tasted, that the knowledge of good and evil, as two twins cleaving together, leaped forth into the world. And perhaps this is that doom which Adam fell into of knowing good and evil, that is to say, of knowing good by evil.[4]

Perhaps this is why fallen beings may insist that Eve's 'selfish' desire for independence and knowledge was justified, understanable, indeed praiseworthy, and that Adam's 'unselfish' willingness to face death and damnation with his beloved wife-mistress-child was also justified, understandable, and praiseworthy; even as they may, alternatively, argue precisely the opposite.

If the knowledge of good comes only through knowing evil, perhaps people can know the true value of what they once took for granted only after they have lost it, and therefore the true paradise will always be the one which has been lost. It is only after she feels she has lost him that Eve recognizes her need for Adam. After Adam turns against her, she experiences the terror of loneliness for herself, and so must humbly admit her own need for love and companionship. Eve was the first to fall, and she is also the first to repent and to accept the burden of responsibility for her own actions. In so doing, she breaks the deadlock of mutual accusation and brings the vain contest to an end with an act of humility which amounts to an act, not of humiliation, but of heroism:

> Forsake me not thus, *Adam*, witness Heav'n
> What love sincere, and reverence in my heart
> I bear thee, and unweeting have offended,
> Unhappily deceiv'd; thy suppliant
> I beg, and clasp thy knees; bereave me not,
> Whereon I live, thy gentle looks, thy aid,
> Thy counsel in this uttermost distress,
> My only strength and stay: forlorn of thee,
> Whither shall I betake me, where subsist?
> While yet we live, scarce one short hour perhaps,
> Between us two let there be peace, both joining,
> As join'd in injuries, one enmity

[4] See Milton's *Areopagitica* in *Complete Poems and Major Prose*, p. 728.

> Against a Foe by doom express assign'd us,
> That cruel Serpent: On me exercise not
> Thy hatred for this misery befall'n,
> On me already lost, mee than thyself
> More miserable; both have sinn'd, but thou
> Against God only, I against God and thee,
> And to the place of judgment will return,
> There with my cries importune Heaven, that all
> The sentence from thy head remov'd may light
> On me, sole cause to thee of all this woe,
> Mee mee only just object of his ire.   (x. 914–36)[5]

In a sense, Eve yet again adopts a 'masculine' attitude even as she kneels before her husband: she offers to assume full responsibility for the actions and obligations of her partner, to take the burden of guilt upon herself. Inspired by her heroic gesture, Adam reciprocates in kind:

>   If Prayers
> Could alter high Decrees, I to that place
> Would speed before thee, and be louder heard,
> That on my head all might be visited,
> Thy frailty and infirmer Sex forgiv'n,
> To me committed and by me expos'd.
> But rise, let us no more contend, nor blame
> Each other, blam'd enough elsewhere, but strive
> In offices of Love, how we may light'n
> Each others burden.   (x. 952–61)

It was divine power that broke the deadlock between the warring angels in heaven, but it is human love that breaks the deadlock between Adam and Eve by transcending it. Their reconciliation also represents a triumph of human reason and freedom alike. Analysing their situation rightly, they freely choose to serve because they freely love; and thus, in the end, they stand together.

In their moments of accepted responsibility, their free decisions to bear the burden of another's guilt, Adam and Eve seem, in all their vulnerable humanity, not less but more heroic than any rebellious archangel. They also seem more heroic than their earlier, innocent, selves, as they walk out of myth into history to make their way, as best they can, in the world we know.

[5] For full discussion of this speech, with its echoes of the Son's heroic speech in Book III, see J. H. Summers, 'The Voice of the Redeemer', in *The Muse's Method: An Introduction to 'Paradise Lost'* (London, 1962), pp. 176–85.

But is this human freedom, this heroism, worth the suffering it entails, worth 'all our woe'? Is what was won worth the cost of what was lost? Yet again, we may debate the pros and cons for ever. Here, for instance, are some arguments in favour of the situation of fallen man:

Milton's epic does indeed justify the ways of God to man. His God stands for freedom, insists upon freedom, and grants freedom even to his adversaries. By leaving Adam and Eve free to choose, free to disobey his own orders, he allows them to grow. Indeed, the very curse imposed upon fallen man, his labour, will finally sustain him: 'Idleness had been worse'. And that last Paradise offered to Adam, a paradise which must be earned, is bound to be 'happier far' than the one which was simply given, and, in the long run, well lost. Eternal life in the garden of innocence might have made man happy had it 'suffic'd him' to have known 'Good by itself, and Evil not at all' (XI. 88–9): but such limited knowledge did not, and could not, suffice. To preserve the happiness of innocence, man would have been forced to confine his thoughts. Only thus could he have obeyed the commandments 'not to know', 'abstain to ask', 'ask not', 'dream not', 'think only what concerns thee' (VII. 120–1, VIII. 173–5). Adam and Eve were right to defy these prohibitions, and God was right to permit them to do so. Though taking into account all its pain, all its penalties, Milton insists that the human condition as it is, not as it might have been, is the ultimate subject for a heroic song that, to the greater glory of God, exalts the 'better fortitude' of mortal man.

And here is a counter-argument based on many of the same quotations:

The condition of mankind would most certainly have been 'happier' had man known 'Good by itself, and Evil not at all' (XI. 88–9). Adam and Eve were wrong to seek forbidden knowledge. Indeed the commandments to 'ask not', and 'dream not', rightly enjoin Adam and Eve to enjoy the present good, the Paradise they actually possess, rather than sacrifice it senselessly for some good which will prove imaginary, some change which will inevitably be for the worse. Far from requiring them to forfeit intellectual freedom, the commandment to 'think only what concerns thee' (VIII. 173–5) in effect requires a realistic and rational assessment of the situation in Paradise, or, in other words, an exercise of intellectual integrity. Thus, in taking the fruit, both Adam and Eve behave in an intellectually, as well as a morally, irresponsible way. They are then expelled from the Paradise of love and innocence into a hostile world where man must labour, grow old, and die; and wherein he is far more likely to create hells within and round about him, than to find that paradise within. The poem is tragic. Whatever man can salvage from the wreckage of his Fall must be of small comfort when it is measured against the glory of the Paradise that was lost.

And so critical interpretations and counter-interpretations may contest with each other, even within an individual reader,[6] since, throughout the epic itself, 'pregnant causes' are so 'mixt' that they 'thus must ever fight' (II. 913-14). 'Good with bad/Expect to hear' (XI. 358-9), says the Archangel Michael, and so says Milton to his audience. Thus, given the vast expanse of Milton's mind; given his ability to take into account those differing, contradictory, truths which yet seem, to the mind that contains them, to be parts of the same truth; given, in short, a poetic vision that looks at life from all sides—it naturally follows that a series of intellectual and poetic arguments as provocative and profound as those in *Paradise Lost* will carry behind them, in their mighty wake, a series of critical controversies that may extend as far into the future as the epic account of the human condition, which cannot but elicit them, will continue to be read.

Indeed, works that create poetic and intellectual deadlocks of one form or another will always be prime sources of critical controversy. Certainly every time a major work of art includes a wicked character (like Satan) who shows attractive qualities (such as energy, intelligence, and courage), that character will inspire critical arguments that the poet was finally on his side: after all, or so one might argue, it is Milton himself who, in the crucial first books, insists upon the 'dauntless courage' and 'immortal vigor' of his fallen archangel. 'And did he smile, his work to see', as he forged the sinews of Satan's heart and framed the fearful symmetry of the Prince of Darkness himself? For that matter, if the poetic imagination can take as much delight in an Iago as an Imogen, a tiger as a lamb, a Satan as an Abdiel, so can, and so should, the imagination of an admirer of poetry. In any case, Milton surely knew that a figure so 'Majestic, though in ruin' could not but inspire pity and terror in an audience that is

---

[6] My final argument here is especially indebted to Frank Kermode's essay 'Adam Unparadis'd' (in *The Living Milton*, pp. 85-123) and to J. H. Summers (op. cit., n. 5, above), p. 175. I once wholeheartedly agreed with Kermode and Summers, but now I am inclined to be partial to my argument in favour of the state of fallen man. Trained in writing his Prolusions (which I imitated here), Milton must have enjoyed presenting powerful arguments for both sides.

encouraged to feel, along with him, Satan's anguish and doubt and fear and sorrow and pain.

Conversely, the same character will inevitably provoke arguments that, because of his immorality, his valour and his suffering count for naught; for it is, after all Milton himself who consistently insists upon Satan's 'obdurate pride', his 'steadfast hate', his 'cruelty', his 'guile', his 'envy', and his specious reasoning.[7] Nowadays, a character of this sort may also inspire arguments that, whereas the poet was never taken in by attractive vice, his readers have been; or that the poet himself intended his readers to be initially taken in, but finally repelled, by sin. Yet a complete view of Satan is not to be found in any single one of these angles of vision.[8] For, in the end, Milton's commitment to tell the whole truth, in all its complexity, defies any critical efforts to insist, exclusively, on only a few, partial truths about a given character or situation.

It is also useful to remember that contests between warring critics will almost always occur when, in any work of art, opposed characters manifest roughly equal, but altogether different, strengths and weaknesses, or virtues and vices. Keats's confrontation between Lamia and Apollonius is an excellent example of such a deadlock: Lamia is beautiful, but an illusion; Apollonius sees true, but his cold, philosophical eye is destructive of poetic beauty. Thus, arguments against Lamia, and for Apollonius, can be countered by arguments against Apollonius, and in favour of Lamia; and all these arguments can be supported, at length, with quotations from the text. So popular are deadlocks with poets, one feels that some of them may have been created for the sheer fun of it, though they may also serve to pose serious aesthetic, moral, or intellectual problems. Here are two obvious examples:

> Safe upon the solid rock the ugly houses stand;
> Come and see my shining palace built upon the sand.

> Whose love is given over well,

---

[7] See Helen Gardner, *A Reading of 'Paradise Lost'* (Oxford, 1965), for a discussion of the complexity of responses evoked by Satan, and an extremely useful distinction between the cosmic movement of the epic, whereby Satan is doomed to lose, and the human level of action, wherein he might be said to win.

[8] My account of responses to Satan is based on those of Blake, Shelley, and their supporters, C. S. Lewis and his supporters, and see also Stanley Fish, *Surprised by Sin: The Reader in 'Paradise Lost'* (London, 1967). As will be seen below, Spenser's 'Bower of Bliss' has evoked strikingly similar critical responses.

Shall gaze on Helen's face in Hell.
Whilst they whose love is thin and wise
May view John Knox in Paradise.[9]

A superb example of a dramatic deadlock occurs in Shakespeare's *Richard II*: the first half of the play stresses the case against Richard and in favour of Bolingbroke, while the second half emphasizes the arguments against Bolingbroke and in favour of Richard. Thus, when Bolingbroke is the underdog, he wins the audience's sympathy, but when he wins the crown, he loses the sympathy to Richard, who, to complete the circle, wins sympathy and admiration only after he loses the crown. Whenever opposed characters of this stature each elicit both admiration and criticism, critical arguments and counter-arguments in favour of one and against the other are bound to follow. Yet the most interesting thing to do, in such cases, may be to acknowledge the deadlock, and go on from there to discuss its implications, to ask how and why the conundrum was created. For this reason, it is worth looking at the deadlock created by a single stanza in Book II of *The Faerie Queene*—a stanza without which the 'Bower of Bliss' episode would seem nothing like so controversial.

In his description of Acrasia's bower, Spenser emphasizes its great beauty and, simultaneously, he insists that its beauty is destructive, evil, and terribly dangerous.[10] The bower is, at once, exalted and criticized as Guyon, the Knight of Temperance, enters to destroy it. So there is a serious complication from the outset: the glory of the bower is as undeniable as its obvious excesses, its superficiality, and its power to destroy human reason. Very natural and powerful moral and aesthetic responses to the situation are, therefore, from the very beginning, set at odds. Yet so long as Guyon himself remains free from any criticism, there is no serious problem so far as Spenser's moral conclusion is concerned. The moral argument of the episode might seem rather pat and obvious, but it would, at least, be absolutely straightforward: glorious, yet

[9] The couplet is by Edna St. Vincent Millay. The classic 'Partial Comfort' is, of course, by Dorothy Parker.

[10] C. S. Lewis, *The Allegory of Love* (Oxford, 1932), pp. 324-6, 330-3, condemns the artificiality of the bower in contrast with the garden of Adonis. For discussions of the bower from different points of view, see A. D. S. Fowler, 'Emblems of Temperance in *The Faerie Queene*, Book II', *Review of English Studies* n.s., 2 (1960), 143-9; and Harry Berger, Jr., *The Allegorical Temper: Vision and Reality in Book II of Spenser's 'Faerie Queen'* (New Haven, 1967).

destructive, sensuality should be brought to terms by temperance. Then, suddenly, Spenser himself inserts a stanza wherein temperance takes the form of a tempestuous and brutally destructive rage:

> But all those pleasant bowres and Pallace braue,
>   *Guyon* broke downe, with rigour pittilesse;
> Ne ought their goodly workmanship might saue
> Them from the tempest of his wrathfulnesse,
> But that their blisse he turn'd to balefulnesse:
> Their groues he feld, their gardins did deface,
> Their arbers spoyle, their Cabinets suppresse,
> Their banket houses burne, their buildings race,
> And of the fairest late, now made the fowlest place.
>
> (II. xii. 83)

Why does Guyon go so far? The source of all the danger in the garden, the sorceress Acrasia, has already been captured. And why does Spenser describe the destruction of the bower in terms of such oppositions as these?

pleasant bowers	—	rigour pitiless
goodly workmanship	—	tempest of wrathfulness
bliss	—	balefulness
groves	—	felled
garden	—	defaced
arbors	—	spoiled
cabinets	—	suppressed
banquet houses	—	burned
buildings	—	razed
what was the fairest place	—	now is the foulest place

Had he wished, Spenser surely could have shown the triumph of temperance over sensuality without making temperance itself turn into a pitiless fury that is out to burn, to spoil, to deface.[11] In this stanza at least, lovely and harmless works of art and nature are ruined by what seems a kind of immorality, a self-righteous indulgence in sheer destruction for its own sake. Indeed, the column of words describing Guyon's actions suggests repression manifesting itself in violence.

In his description of Acrasia's bower and Guyon's destruction

---

[11] For further problems with the ideal of Temperance, see Howard Erskine-Hill, 'Antony and Octavius: The Theme of Temperance in Shakespeare's *Antony and Cleopatra*', *Renaissance and Modern Studies*, 14 (1970), 26–47.

of it Spenser thus creates a poetic deadlock. Describing the bower, he shows that beauty, poetry, and sensuality may lead their admirers, like the admirers of Acrasia, into dangerous and deadly excesses, and that the slavishly sensual life is a bestial one; Grille for ever remains a pig. Yet as he describes the wrecking of the bower, Spenser shows that puritanical assaults on beauty, poetry, art, and sensuality may themselves take the form of excess: Guyon's behaviour is comparable to that of a Savonarola.

Of course, independently of this stanza, Guyon should be allowed to score his series of unanswerably valid moral points. But, again independently of this stanza, Spenser himself has chosen to bless Acrasia's bower with the equally unanswerable arguments of poetry. Indeed, it is in his magnificent description of his glorious, dangerous strumpet, sparkling in beauty and destruction too, that Spenser achieves the union of imagination with nature which, in Constable's words, is the 'whole object and difficulty'[12] of art:

> Vpon a bed of Roses she was layd,
>   As faint through heat, or dight to pleasant sin,
>   And was arayd, or rather disarayd,
>   All in a vele of silke and siluer thin,
>   That hid no whit her alablaster skin,
>   But rather shewd more white, if more might bee:
>   More subtile web *Arachne* cannot spin,
>   Nor the fine nets, which oft we wouen see
> Of scorched deaw, do not in th'aire more lightly flee.

> Her snowy brest was bare to readie spoyle
>   Of hungry eies, which n'ote therewith be fild,
>   And yet through languour of her late sweet toyle,
>   Few drops, more cleare than Nectar, forth distild,
>   That like pure Orient perles adowne it trild,
>   And her faire eyes sweet smyling in delight,
>   Moystened their fierie beames, with which she thrild
>   Fraile harts, yet quenched not; like starry light
> Which sparckling on the silent waues, does seeme more bright.
>
>   (II. xii. 77, 78)

'Oh, rare for Antony!' Agrippa exclaimed when Enobarbus described Cleopatra's appearance on the river Cydnus. And 'how rare for Verdant!' is surely one obvious response to Spenser's

---

[12] Constable is quoted by E. H. Gombrich in *Art and Illusion*, p. 329.

description of Acrasia. It could, of course, be argued that Shake-speare's coldly politic Octavius, like Guyon, represents the triumphant virtues of temperance which inevitably win out over the self-destructive forms of excess preferred by Antony and Cleopatra. 'But so what?' one might snap back; 'The priorities acted upon by Antony and Cleopatra were, after all, their own; they were true to themselves; and if Octavius condemns them, they, in turn, despise him.' And so far as Acrasia's lover, Verdant, is concerned, we might well wonder whether he himself would consider Guyon's 'counsell sage' a satisfactory substitute for Acrasia's embraces. In connection with Grille and Verdant (and Antony and Cleopatra), one is inclined to think of the old Englishman, in *Out of Africa*, who was described in La Belle Otéro's memoirs as a young man who had squandered his entire fortune on her, but who had received 'full value' for it. To the obvious question posed him by Karen Blixen, 'And do you consider . . . that you did have full value?', the old gentleman, after pausing for only a very short moment to think, answered, 'Yes. Yes, I had.'[13]

In what, one hopes, is a desperate effort to squelch such responses in favour of passion, sensuality, and excess, it has been argued that Spenser is a kind of pious pornographer, who deliberately arouses his readers in order, subsequently, to show them up as a pack of libidinous wolves. According to this theory, 'the reader' is all too easily seduced by Spenser's sensuous images. Then, properly chagrined at his own preference for the 'intemperate life', he is forced into an 'embarrassing confrontation' with his own 'basic concupiscence'.[14] But what if 'the reader' is not in

---

[13] *Out of Africa*, p. 225.

[14] Quotations are from Arlene N. Okerlund, 'Spenser's Wanton Maidens: Reader Psychology in the Bower of Bliss', *PMLA* 88 (1973), 62–8. Some of my arguments here were published in a letter to the editor of the *PMLA* 'Forum' (Oct. 1973), 1185–7. In her reply to my letter (pp. 1187–8 of the same issue), Okerlund argues that we cannot have things both ways; we cannot consider Guyon the hero of Book II and, simultaneously, reject his final act in destroying the bower. Why on earth not? If we were to follow her line of reasoning, we could not consider Othello the 'hero' of *Othello* and still deplore his murder of Desdemona. Okerlund also adds that 'other than to point out a set of values that differ from the poet's' or a 'change in historical attitudes' our own preferences are quite irrelevant. Then whose *are* relevant? Spenser's original audience has been mouldering in the grave for some years now. Furthermore, Okerlund's essay was supposed to be about 'Reader Psychology' and surely, as a 'reader', my 'psychological' response to Guyon's destruction of the bower is as 'relevant' as the next 'reader's'. Of *course* I may be wrong here; but, then, so may Okerlund. I did not insert the disturbing stanza, nor am I the first to notice the

the least surprised, nor embarrassed, nor chagrined by his (or her) basic concupiscence? For that matter, if all we can gain from reading Spenser's poem is a recognition of our own 'intemperate desires', why should we waste time with it? Given any understanding of human biology and psychology, one hardly need turn to *The Faerie Queene* to recognize one's own, perfectly normal, susceptibility to lust. Be that as it may, the theory that Spenser is out to expose the intemperate concupiscence of his readers could be instantly countered by the dialectically opposite, and equally defensible, theory that, for Spenser and his readers alike,

> The moral sense in mortals is the duty
> We have to pay on mortal sense of beauty.

Surely one might better conclude that 'the reader's' ambivalent responses to Guyon's righteous, but pitiless, destruction of the bower, and to Acrasia's beautiful, but destructive, sensuality, rightly reflect Spenser's accurate presentation of the problems and dangers involved in leading an exclusively temperate life, just as they rightly reflect Spenser's powerful portrayal of the problems and dangers inherent in the excessively sensual life. For though it can be argued that Spenser sharply rebukes his audience for having assisted at an aesthetic performance when it should have been judging a moral one, he also makes clear that a puritanical insistence on temperance-in-all-things is by its very nature at emnity with even those harmless forms of beauty, poetry, imagination, art, and sensuality that, by their very nature, involve a fine excess.

His duty to tell the truth about human experience would appear to have obliged this moral poet to present cases for and against his villainess and hero alike. Like Milton, Spenser gives his very devils their due. In short, he permits us to 'see and know': whether or not we choose to 'abstain' remains our own affair. And it is, perhaps, because he supplies grounds for criticism of his hero and, simultaneously, glorifies and condemns his villainess that Spenser's account of the Bower of Bliss has survived as a living likeness of truth rather than a long-abandoned monument to dead

---

'vindictive' hostility in it—see, for instance, Paul J. Alpers, *The Poetry of 'The Faerie Queene'* (Princeton, N.J., 1967), pp. 305–6. No one knows for sure why Spenser made it so violent, and we can go on arguing about its effect for the rest of our lives. That is the point of this chapter.

ideas. Certainly his mighty opposites, Acrasia and Guyon, are far more than 'teaching devices' that 'point a finger of accusation' directly at the reader who succumbs to 'carnal lust'. Like the poem in which they appear, they point in many directions other than that one. They point in the direction of Circe, and in the direction of Savonarola; they point towards Shakespeare's wanton but glorious Cleopatra, and towards his virtuous but dull Octavia; they point towards Comus and the Lady; they point towards Lamia and Apollonius. They point upward in the direction of moral idealism, and downward in the direction of human biology; they point outward towards poetry and music and magic, and straight ahead in the direction of ordinary experience. We shall never be done discussing them.

Looking back at the Bower of Bliss from this distance, it seems significant that poetry itself has, over the centuries, been critically attacked for reasons markedly similar to those which caused Guyon to destroy Acrasia's bower: like Acrasia, poetry has been condemned for its power to enchant, to inflame base and intemperate desires, to make 'sin' seem 'pleasant', and so seduce men from their proper duties to themselves and to others. Like the art of Acrasia's garden, the art of poetry has been condemned for its essential artificiality,[15] its unreality. Yet poetry has also been considered a form of forbidden fruit, a source of that knowledge of some good, or some evil, which political and moral authorities have insisted that men would be better off without. Nevertheless, the greatest poets persist in telling the truth about human experience, regardless of what any 'moralists' (or dictators) may tell them they ought to have done; and the attack on the immorality of poetry still goes on.

For instance, if certain twentieth-century critical essays were the only ones to survive into the twenty-fifth century, the scholar who discovered them might decide that they were our equivalent of sermons; that the duty of criticism was, in our era, deemed to

---

[15] The 'art' of Acrasia's bower and Spenser's own art of poetry are, in fact, one and the same. See R. M. Adams, *Proteus, His Lies, His Truth* (New York, 1973), p. 79: whereas C. S. Lewis 'would persuade us that the wedding of art and nature in the Bower of Bliss should be read as an indictment of the whole place as false and unnatural . . . one might want to keep an open attitude here towards a process which seems to be the process of the poem itself'. For that matter, G. Wilson Knight concludes that '*The Faerie Queene* is itself one vast Bower of Bliss'—see 'The Spenserian Fluidity', reprinted in *Edmund Spenser*, ed. Paul J. Alpers (Harmondsworth, 1969), pp. 222–32—the quotation is from p. 228.

be a demonstration of the critic's moral superiority to literary characters, and, occasionally, the assertion of his moral superiority to the creators of those characters as well. The twenty-fifth-century reader of, say, H. A. Mason's *Shakespeare's Tragedies of Love* or A. L. French's *Shakespeare and the Critics* will be constantly warned not to be taken in by the enchanting verses describing, or spoken by, among others, Othello, Hamlet, and Antony; it will be repeatedly pointed out to him that Shakespeare himself sometimes failed to get his moral bearings straight; and he will be instructed, by example, that the proper critical attitude towards works of art, characters, and artists alike should be one of moral 'rigour pitilesse'.[16]

But might not that twenty-fifth-century reader finally conclude that any impassioned arguments insisting that he ought not to be taken in by poetry, or characters, or poets, are somewhat ludicrous? For who could possibly be more 'taken in' by characters, poetry, and poets than one who has spent hours and hours, days and days, weeks and weeks, or even years and years, writing tirades against the vices and follies of imaginary beings who, at their very worst, but poison in jest, no harm in the world?

Yet the peculiar paradox posed here is not, itself, a ludicrous one. Indeed, all literary criticism, from the best to the worst, derives from a fundamental and profound problem: how can the human intellect properly evaluate products of the human imagination? Indeed, the very same question arises, with striking frequency, within many major works of art; certainly it seems to have haunted Shakespeare. It may never be satisfactorily solved. But it can, perhaps, be best discussed by looking at a series of plays that explicitly show how difficult it is to be certain whether the insights of one's own imagination are honest ghosts or juggling fiends.

[16] See, for instance, French on *Hamlet* (quoted above, p. 21); and Mason (cited above, p. 27) on *Othello*: 'The story needed rounding out with a return to Venice and a sentence of banishment. Othello was *rightly* killed in Cinthio's tale by the kinsmen of Desdemona. Keeping to the play, we may be sorry that Gratiano does not catch Emilia's fire and hold a moral mirror up to Othello giving him one last chance to see himself as he was' (p. 135). See also p. 74, where Mason concludes that the 'facile, painless' oppositions between Iago's 'cynicism' and Othello's 'sentimentalism' have 'the effect of making us blush for Shakespeare and the reach-me-down world of "Theatre business, management of men" in which *Othello* no doubt had to be composed.'

IV

'If this be error': Imagination and truth in Shakespeare and Marlowe

But men may construe things after their fashion,
Clean from the purpose of the things themselves.
                        CICERO in *Julius Caesar*

My thoughts and my discourse as madmen's are,
At random from the truth vainly express'd;
For I have sworn thee fair and thought thee bright
Who art as black as hell, as dark as night.
                        SHAKESPEARE, *Sonnet 147*

'DOES a firm persuasion that a thing is so, make it so?' Plays by Shakespeare and Marlowe provide two different answers to Blake's question. So far as a firm persuasion about one's own nature or potential is concerned, the answer they give, as we shall see later, is 'Yes'. Certain people may indeed become what they believe themselves to be, or what they once only imagined they might become. But so far as realities external to ourselves are concerned, the answer is 'No'. The intensity of conviction with which a theory is believed to be true has no bearing upon its validity except in so far as it produces a proportionately strong inducement to find out whether it is true or not. For no force of the human intellect or imagination can alter a natural law, or a situation, or a personality which exists, in its own right, independently of the imagination which perceives and interprets it. Not even Tamburlaine, who made all his dreams of power and glory come true, could stop Death from taking his Zenocrate, make himself live a week longer, or transform his son into his own likeness. No power of the will can 'call back yesterday, bid time return'. Nor can a firm persuasion that it is so, transform faithless love into true.

Given his firm persuasion that she would be true to him, when Shakespeare's Troilus sees his adored Cressida throwing herself at Diomedes, he can only conclude that this cannot be *his* Cressida:

> This she? no, this is Diomed's Cressida:
> If beauty have a soul, this is not she;
> If souls guide vows, if vows be sanctimonies,
> If sanctimony be the gods' delight,
> If there be rule in unity itself,
> This is not she.

Yet given the evidence before him, he must needs admit that this is she, that 'this is, and is not, Cressid':[1]

> Instance, O instance! strong as Pluto's gates;
> Cressid is mine, tied with the bonds of heaven:
> Instance, O instance! strong as heaven itself;
> The bonds of heaven are slipp'd, dissolved, and loosed;
> And with another knot, five-finger-tied,
> The fractions of her faith, orts of her love,
> The fragments, scraps, the bits and greasy relics
> Of her o'er-eaten faith, are bound to Diomed.   (v. ii. 137–60)

'Diomed's Cressid' is certainly Cressida herself, but is certainly not Cressida as Troilus imagined her to be. She never was, in fact, as she was valued by him.

When he first meets her, Ulysses instantly recognizes Cressida as a 'daughter of the game'. But until he sees her with Diomedes, Troilus sees her as his fair lady, and imagines his own sexual desire for her to be a romantic quest for a pearl of great price: 'her bed is India; there she lies, a pearl'. His very fantasies of love-making are so potent that Troilus fears anticipation might impede the capacity of his 'ruder powers' to act them out:

> I am giddy; expectation whirls me round.
> The imaginary relish is so sweet
> That it enchants my sense . . . I fear me,
> Swooning destruction, or some joy too fine,
> Too subtle-potent, tuned too sharp in sweetness,
> For the capacity of my ruder powers.   (iii. ii. 19–26)

Cressida herself, of course, knows how to enhance her appeal to

---

[1] Earlier on, Cressida herself tells Troilus,

> I have a kind of self resides with you;
> But an unkind self, that itself will leave,
> To be another's fool.   iii. ii. 155–6)

his imagination. She knows 'Men prize the thing ungain'd more than it is': that is why she deliberately holds off for as long as she does. 'Never did young man fancy' with 'so eternal and fix'd a soul' as Troilus, who was so imaginatively and physically inflamed by her that he equated her beauty with truth, and so created a living goddess from what was, after all, only a pretty girl 'of quick sense'. Thus, as Cressida puts it, the error of the eye directs the mind. And what error leads, must err (v. ii. 110–11).

Here, as elsewhere, Shakespeare demonstrates that the true nature and value of a person, situation, or thing have their own independent realities, quite apart from any and all convictions concerning them. For those convictions may (as the King of France said to Lear) be mingled with regards that stand aloof from the entire point:

> *Troilus.*   What is aught, but as 'tis valued?
> *Hector.*   But value dwells not in particular will;
> It holds his estimate and dignity
> As well wherein 'tis precious of itself
> As in the prizer: 'tis mad idolatry
> To make the service greater than the god;
> And the will dotes that is attributive
> To what infectiously itself affects,
> Without some image of the affected merit.   (ii. ii. 52–60)

As a different play demonstrates, and as the King of France also realized, his bride's value dwelt in herself, and not in the way she was valued by others: the 'unpriz'd, precious' Cordelia was 'herself a dowry'. Therefore, while the human imagination is inevitably subjective, there is such a thing as truth, as an objective reality against which any subjective interpretations of it may themselves be evaluated. 'Truth is truth to the end of reckoning.' The truth, however, may be hard to come by—especially when an error of the eye directs the mind. The eyes of doting love, for instance, can lead one to admire, with utter rapture, the furry splendour of some beloved ass's ears, or they can invest a Cressida with the qualities of a Desdemona. Conversely the eyes of jealousy can shape 'faults that are not', and so persuade the mind that a Desdemona, or a Hermione, was as false as Cressida.

'Too hot, too hot!' says Leontes, as he watches his beautiful, pregnant, wife urge Polixenes to postpone his parting from them

for a while. At this precise moment in *The Winter's Tale* (1. ii. 108),
Leontes apprehends what he believes to be the truth. In a lightning flash of insight he is persuaded that Hermione and Polixenes
are in love, that they have been lovers for a long time, and that the
child his wife is carrying is the child of his rival. He is appalled by
this new 'knowledge'; he is tormented by it. Yet he is absolutely
convinced of its validity:

> How blest am I
> In my just censure, in my true opinion!
> Alack, for lesser knowledge! how accursed
> In being so blest! There may be in the cup
> A spider steep'd, and one may drink, depart,
> And yet partake no venom, for his knowledge
> Is not infected: but if one present
> The abhorr'd ingredient to his eye, make known
> How he hath drunk, he cracks his gorge, his sides,
> With violent hefts. I have drunk, and seen the spider.
>
> (II. i. 36–45)

Leontes does not attempt to judge his own conviction critically.
Instead, he concentrates on proving Hermione guilty. Until the
death of his son is announced, he sees only what is illuminated by
the revolving searchlights of his jealousy. He therefore admits
every shred of evidence which confirms his theory, and imperiously
dismisses all efforts to refute it:

> . . . if you, or stupefied
> Or seeming so in skill, cannot or will not
> Relish a truth like us, inform yourselves
> We need no more of your advice.   (II. i. 165–8)

Thus Leontes persistently clings to, and even seems to 'relish',
his supremely painful 'truth'. For the sake of it, he does not hesitate
to sacrifice the lives of others, or, for that matter, to throw away
his own happiness. His passionate adherence to what he believes
to be true costs him his wife and daughter for sixteen years, and
it costs the life of his only son, for ever.

Still, given Leontes's point of view, his theory was a tenable
one. It might have been true. It explained a lot. Looking for confirmations, Leontes found them in the pregnancy of Hermione,
the flight of Polixenes, and the escape of Camillo. The counter-
arguments by Antigonus and other courtiers could merely have

demonstrated, as Leontes thought they did, that he was surrounded by traitors, who had some personal stake in their refusals to admit the truth. In these terms, Leontes's 'firm persuasion' is typical of many theories to which human beings have clung tenaciously, and for which they have, upon occasion, sacrificed their own happiness and the lives of their children. Such theories have in common the effect of a conversion or revelation which opens the eyes to some truth hidden from those not yet initiated. They also serve to explain everything that happens within the fields to which they refer. Thus, once the eyes have been opened by a revelation of this kind, the world seems full of evidence that confirms its validity. Its truth appears manifest to its adherents, while critics of the theory are held to be infidels who do not want to admit the truth, or who refuse to see it, or who have some vested interest in rejecting it.[2]

And yet, as the verdicts of the oracle demonstrate, even the most deeply held convictions, the most 'manifest' truths, may prove false: Hermione was chaste; Polixenes blameless; Camillo a true subject; and the innocent babe truly begotten (III. ii. 133–5). Apollo's verdicts also serve to refute any arguments that, because all interpretations are equally subjective, they are all equally valid. Paulina's faith in Hermione's innocence was just as subjective, and quite as passionately maintained, as Leontes's conviction of her guilt; but Paulina's interpretation of the situation did, in fact, correspond to the facts. And, like Paulina's pleas, surely the death of Leontes's other innocent child, Mamilius, suggests that people had better put their own brain-children to some very severe tests before sacrificing any real children for their sakes. For while our own brain-children may indeed turn out to be true Cordelias, they may also be Gonerils and Regans, to whom we give everything, but who will, after taking it, turn on us and mock us. One thinks of Kent's frantic warnings to Lear, and of Crom-

---

[2] See K. R. Popper, *Conjectures and Refutations*, pp. 34–6. It is easy, Popper concludes, to obtain confirmation, or verifications, for any number of theories—that is, if we look only for confirmations. This is certainly true of theories about literature. One very real danger to literary criticism is the tendency to verify arguments by seeking to apply and to confirm them, even to the point of neglecting refutations. See A. N. Kaul, *The Action of English Comedy* (New Haven, 1970), p. 1: 'I am only too conscious of all that I have left out, both by way of what could have been accommodated within my general argument but was not and by way of what simply could not be fitted into that argument without subjecting it to severe dislocation and even disproof.'

well's warning to the General Assembly, 'I beseech you, in the bowels of Christ, think it possible you may be mistaken'.

In contrast to Leontes, who refused to acknowledge any evidence against his own 'true opinion', Hamlet considers himself obliged to seek out evidence against the insights of his own 'prophetic soul'. Even though he is prompted to his revenge by heaven and hell, and though he hates, loathes, and despises the bloody, bawdy, treacherous, lecherous, kindless King of Denmark with all his heart, Hamlet decides to subject the spectral evidence against his uncle to a critical test. He will expose his own conjectures to refutation by an objective experiment. He will test the evidence of one illusion, a Ghost, against the evidence produced by another illusion, a play. He will, in short, set the imagination to catch the imagination:

> The spirit that I have seen
> May be the devil: and the devil hath power
> To assume a pleasing shape; yea, and perhaps
> Out of my weakness and my melancholy,
> As he is very potent with such spirits,
> Abuses me to damn me: I'll have grounds
> More relative than this: the play's the thing
> Wherein I'll catch the conscience of the King.

(II. ii. 627–34)

If Claudius's 'occulted guilt' does not manifest itself, then Hamlet will himself admit that his own 'imaginations' were 'as foul as Vulcan's stithy' (III. ii. 85–9).[3] It is only after the King's haunted memory does indeed prompt him to start, like a guilty thing

---

[3] Hamlet's method of seeking to falsify his own theory is, by all odds, more truly 'scientific' than Leontes's interest only in confirmations. See P. B. Medawar, *Induction and Intuition in Scientific Thought* (London, 1969), p. 46: 'The process by which we come to formulate a hypothesis is not illogical but non-logical, i.e. outside logic. But once we have formed an opinion we can expose it to criticism, usually by experimentation . . . "If our hypothesis is sound," we say, "if we have taken the right view, then it follows that . . ."—and we then take steps to find out whether what follows logically is indeed the case.' If our predictions are borne out, then we are justified in 'extending a certain confidence to the hypothesis'. If not, 'there must be something wrong, perhaps so wrong as to oblige us to abandon our hypothesis altogether.' The history of criticism is full of attempts to provide objective, experimental, 'scientific', tests by which works of art, and critical theories about them, may be *proved* good or flawed, right or wrong. But there are no certain tests. Time seems as good as any test of art, and it represents the cumulative and subjective verdict of individual readers and spectators over centuries. And if no one agrees with the critic's 'firm persuasion' that *Hamlet* is a miserable failure there is nothing he can do to prove his case: 'If the King like not the [tragedy,] why then, belike, he likes it not, pardy.'

surprised, that Hamlet can 'take the ghost's word for a thousand pound' (III. ii. 296–7).

Much of what happens in *Hamlet* involves efforts to sound out the mysteries of others, to verify what people imagine to be true about others. 'Who's there?'; 'What are they doing?'; 'Why are they doing it?'; 'Who did it?'; 'Did they do it?'; 'How *could* they do it'—these are questions which reverberate through the royal castle at Elsinore.[4] Horatio suspects that the Ghost is but a fantasy, and goes up on the parapet to see for himself. Polonius imagines that Hamlet is suffering from lover's melancholy, and tries to test that idea. Claudius sends for Rosencrantz and Guildenstern to ferret out the reasons behind Hamlet's unusual behaviour. Laertes seeks to know the certainty behind his own father's death, and Hamlet himself is determined to find out whether or not his own assumptions correspond to the facts. Some of these efforts prove futile: Polonius is convinced that his theory is confirmed, and Rosencrantz and Guildenstern seem to conclude that Hamlet is motivated by ambition. But Hamlet, who was willing to change his mind, should the evidence so require, does learn that whatever else it might be, the apparition he saw on the parapet was indeed an 'honest Ghost'. So one can, if one likes, chart the way certain knowledge about the original murder, combined with a certain knowledge that certain knowledge is possessed by others, alters the relationships between the central characters in *Hamlet*. In the beginning, only Claudius and the Ghost know the truth; then Hamlet and Horatio learn that Claudius killed Hamlet's father; Claudius then knows that Hamlet knows, and Hamlet knows that Claudius knows he knows, while Claudius knows that Hamlet knows he knows he knows, and so on, in a whirligig worthy of R. D. Laing, until finally Horatio, having survived beyond the tragedy's end, will report Hamlet's cause aright to the unsatisfied, and everyone will know. Like ghosts, foul deeds may rise, though all the world o'erwhelm them, to men's eyes.

And like other dramatic ghosts that haunt plays by Ibsen, Strindberg, and Yeats, the ghost in *Hamlet* can be seen as a symbolic manifestation of some truth about the past which cannot be

---

[4] The 'interrogative mood' dominates the rhetoric of *Hamlet*. See Maynard Mack, 'The World of Hamlet', reprinted in *Shakespeare: Modern Essays in Criticism*, ed. Leonard F. Dean (New York, 1961), pp. 237–57, I am specially indebted to this essay throughout this chapter.

permanently suppressed: 'Remember me!' it urgently, repeatedly, insists. And, indeed, from beginning to end, this particular tragedy is obsessed by the remembrance of things past, by the *status quo ante*. This helps explain why, here—perhaps more than anywhere else—Shakespeare deliberately introduces names and incidents which have little to do with the immediate situation, but which extend the lives of certain characters into a dimension of time and space lying behind and beyond the action portrayed in his play's present.

For instance, he stops all dramatic action for the sake of the following, seemingly irrelevant, discussion:

> *Claudius.* . . . Two months since,
> Here was a gentleman of Normandy:—
> I've seen myself, and served against, the French,
> And they can well on horseback: but this gallant
> Had witchcraft in't; he grew unto his seat;
> And to such wondrous doing brought his horse,
> As he had been incorpsed and demi-natured
> With the brave beast: so far he topp'd my thought,
> That I, in forgery of shapes and tricks,
> Came short of what he did.
> *Laertes.* A Norman was't?
> *Claudius.* A Norman.
> *Laertes.* Upon my life, Lamond.
> *Claudius.* The very same.
> *Laertes.* I know him well: he is the brooch indeed
> And gem of all the nation. (IV. vii. 82–95)

Claudius and Laertes thus discover a mutual acquaintance, unknown to us, but known to them quite independently of their actions in *Hamlet*. We are also supplied, here, with the useless information that Claudius once fought against the French, just as, elsewhere, we are quite as gratuitously informed that Polonius once acted the part of Julius Caesar. Then, of course, later on we learn that there was a court jester named Yorick who once held the young Prince Hamlet on his shoulders:

> Alas, poor Yorick! I knew him, Horatio: a fellow
> of infinite jest, of most excellent fancy: he hath
> borne me on his back a thousand times. (V. i. 291–4)

There was, we are told, a time when Hamlet was the glass of fashion and the mould of form, the sweet rose of the State of

Denmark. That was when he courted Ophelia, and wrote her love letters and little poems. There was a time when Gertrude hung on Hamlet's father as if her appetite for him had grown by what it fed on. There was a time when Rosencrantz and Guildenstern were excellent good friends to Hamlet, and when a boy actor was by the altitude of a chopine shorter than when he played the Player-Queen.

For Hamlet himself, the doors to the past, to old friendships, old love, and old certainties, are closed. Characters in this ghost-ridden play seem to be wraiths, or perversions of their former selves. Rosencrantz and Guildenstern, Hamlet's old friends, now spy for his enemy. Gertrude, so loving to Hamlet's father, now honeys and makes love with his murderer. Hamlet, who loved Ophelia, treats her rudely and cruelly. There is a possible point here: the people of our youth change, like us, with ambition, marriage, children, age, and can no longer be trusted, any more than we can. Their old selves, and our old selves, seem to be dead and buried, and yet, as spectres, may haunt us still. Be that as it may, the ghosts of times past that pass back and forth through the doors of memory—Yorick, Lamond, images of the good old days —somehow help make it possible for us, in Shakespeare's audience, to remember Hamlet and his world even better than we might remember the real Lamonds, Yoricks, and Guildensterns we knew in the world which we ourselves inhabited at the time we first read this tragedy. On a second reading of the play, and even more so on a twenty-second reading, one recognizes its characters as old acquaintances, old enemies, and old friends. One may, with Claudius and Laertes, remember that Lamond was an excellent horseman. One can exchange gossip about Gertrude, precisely as if she were a mutual acquaintance, with someone met casually, only five minutes before, at some party.

And so, images from the past filter through this tragedy in much the same way that images from *Hamlet* may filter through one's own memory in real life. Like ghosts, they intrude suddenly upon the present. Yet that long-forgotten jester grimaces from the grave to remind us all that there is no going back to times past except in memory.[5]

[5] Or in art. However we ourselves may have changed since we last read the play, we can return to the world of *Hamlet* and find it unchanged; though, of course, how *we* have changed may radically alter its meaning for us, as individuals.

But there is also no pretending that the truths of the past can, at will, be effectively suppressed or denied. One's buried truths may be tragic, but there is no way of being certain that they will not, for the bane and the enlightenment of the present, break loose from their confines. Thus the past may exert great pressures on the present and so influence the future. And, surely, the influence of the Ghost of Hamlet's father[6] is analogous to the pressures exerted upon the present by the past. 'He who fights the future', said Kierkegaard, 'has a dangerous enemy', and, as Claudius learns for himself, the same may be said of those who fight the past. Claudius, of course, had determined that the truth about the past would remain buried for ever; poor passionate Gertrude, in her futile efforts to make the best of the present, fatally failed to remember the past; and Hamlet tried to find out the whole truth before he acted on what he thought that truth might be. And he did find out the truth. By the end of the tragedy, Claudius's original sin, his guilt, his most pernicious murder of Hamlet's father, are shown to be realities as undeniable as the innocence of Hermione. 'The King's to blame' for the carnage at the end, as well.[7]

[6] For a convenient survey of theories about the Ghost, see John Jump, 'Shakespeare's Ghosts', *Critical Quarterly*, 12 (1970), 339–51, and Eleanor Prosser, *Hamlet and Revenge* (Stanford, Calif., 1971), pp. 100–1. This book is full of quotations from Elizabethan sources, but Prosser's claim to be more 'objective' about *Hamlet* than her predecessors in investigations of Elizabethan notions concerning revenge and ghosts is irritating, since she is no more objective than anyone else. For instance, she cites James Drake's *The Antient and Modern Stages Survey'd* (1699) in support of her argument about Ophelia (p. 150), but apparently did not notice that Drake, quite at odds with her own theory, takes it for granted that the Ghost is, in fact, the 'late King's Ghost' (Drake, p. 203). I find Prosser's throwing of quotations from Elizabethan moralists at each other, and at the reader, something of a waste of time. The only way, say, to find out what Elizabethans *really* thought about revenge would be to go through all court records and see what juries actually did about men charged with murdering the murderers of their fathers, wives, children, brothers, etc. I remember watching a trial resulting from a vendetta that had claimed four lives already— brothers shooting brothers who shot brothers, as a result of a practical joke played decades earlier, in the 1930s, when one set of brothers put sugar in the petrol tank of a precious car belonging to another set of brothers. Not one of the revengers was given anything like the severe sentence required by the state. They all got off, because the jurors (who were probably as 'God-fearing' as their Elizabethan counterparts) were sympathetic. They themselves might have done the same thing. If it can be argued that this case is 'regional' and 'special' it can be argued that all cases of private revenge are regional and 'special'. Anyway, Elizabethan court records would provide a more authentic test of historically held attitudes than any amount of quotations from moralists.

[7] See Drake (*The Antient and Modern Stages Survey'd*, pp. 204–6) for the theory that the crime and punishment of Claudius are central throughout the play. *Hamlet* is, he

Yet the facts of the case, the truth behind what appeared to be a very mysterious death, and an equally mysterious scene of slaughter, finally seem as plain as day compared with the mysteries of the human personality which were involved in various efforts to suppress, to ignore, or to discover the facts. The evidence against Claudius could be proved true or false: so we can know, first by means of a shade, and then beyond the shadow of a doubt, that Claudius killed his brother: 'O, my offence is rank', he tells us, 'it smells to heaven'; it has the 'primal eldest curse' upon it, 'A brother's murder'. But we cannot know why Claudius could not pray—not even Claudius himself knows that (III. iii. 64–71, 97–8). 'That which you are', Hamlet seems to conclude, as he gazes on Ophelia's face, 'my thoughts cannot transpose'. Ophelia herself will never know why she was treated so cruelly. And Hamlet can never know that, whereas most of his firm persuasions about Claudius were valid, some of them were wrong: though his act of prayer had no 'relish of salvation' in it at all, Claudius was not 'remorseless'.

Thus, while on one level both Hamlet and his play are concerned with avenging a murder, they are also concerned with what human beings are capable of imagining and knowing about others, and with what they are capable of imagining and knowing about themselves. Certain truths are, of course, learned by the various characters: our thoughts are ours, their ends none of our own; our indiscretion sometimes serves us well, when our dear plots do pall. Certain criminal actions will finally appear in their true nature. But no one either in Hamlet or watching it can, in effect, know the truth which lies at the heart of the individual human personality:

Hamlet. Why, look you now, how unworthy a thing you make of me! You would play upon me; you would seem to know my stops; you would pluck out the heart of my mystery; you would sound me from my lowest note to the top of my compass . . . 'Sblood, do you think that I am easier to be played on than a pipe? Call me what instrument you will, though you can fret me, yet you cannot play upon me.

(III. ii. 379–89)

Like Rosencrantz, Guildenstern, Claudius, and Gertrude, many people who have participated, as spectators, at Hamlet's tragedy

---

says, an account of 'Murther privately committed, strangely discover'd, and wonderfully punish'd'.

have, over the centuries, tried to 'know Hamlet's stops', but they, too, have failed to pluck out the heart of his mystery. Indeed, Solzhenitsyn's discussion of Dostoevsky's unfathomable characters applies, with special validity, to Hamlet:

> 'Well, say—how are we to understand the character of Stavrogin?'
> 'But there are dozens of critical studies! . . .'
> '. . . I've read them all. Stavrogin! Svidrigailov! Kirillov! Nobody understands them. They are as complex, as unpredictable as only people in real life can be. We hardly ever understand a person at first sight, and we never understand them right through. Something unexpected always turns up. That's just where Dostoyevsky is such a genius! And literary critics think they can hold his characters up to the light and see through them. It's comic!'[8]

Perhaps partly because his plays are frequently concerned with what human beings are *not* capable of knowing about themselves or about each other—

> Tell me, Apollo, for thy Daphne's love,
> What Cressid is, what Pandar, and what we?

many of Shakespeare's characters have defied the mightiest critical and scholarly efforts to 'understand them right through'.

Like his great contemporary, Marlowe, Shakespeare also seems to have been concerned with the correspondence, or the lack of it, between what people may imagine themselves to be and what they may become. *Tamburlaine* (Part I), *Dr. Faustus*, and *Macbeth* all show how the dictates of the human imagination, whether true or false, may alter human nature. So far as internal realities are

---

[8] *The First Circle*, trans. Michael Guybon, pp. 460–1. (See also the attack on the scholarly ideal of 'Objectivity' on p. 396.) The endless critical efforts to explain his behaviour testify that Hamlet's character remains something of a mystery to us, even as it remains a mystery to him. 'I do not know why I . . .', he keeps saying. Certainly he has been as admired, and as berated, as any character in Shakespeare. He has, in the past, been criticized because he delayed his revenge, and, more recently, criticized because he wanted to take it. But from a legalistic, literal, point of view, the fact that he considers himself a minister of justice helps account for both the delay and the revenge. Certainly any judge, given the evidence amassed against him, would condemn Claudius. If we are going to damn Hamlet for killing the man who killed his father, on the grounds that God claimed all vengeance was his, then the same divine edict obliges us to damn both the servant who stabbed Cornwall, and Macduff, who killed the man who killed his wife and children: 'Tyrant', says Macduff, 'show thy face!'

> If thou be'st slain and with no stroke of mine,
> My wife and children's ghosts will haunt me still.

concerned, a firm persuasion that a thing is so may, indeed, make it so, even if it was not necessarily so to begin with. Thus people who persistently act on what they imagine themselves to be, may sometimes become what they were once only capable of imagining they might be. They may, in fact, become what they act.

Like Shakespeare, Marlowe knew that 'the very substance of the ambitious is merely the shadow of a dream' (*Hamlet*, II. ii. 264–5). Throughout Tamburlaine's career, the ambitious Scythian shepherd transforms his dreams of earthly kingdoms, power, and glory, into substances. He will not remain in the humble rank into which he was born. What he can imagine being, he will be; what he can imagine having, he will have. However wild, or beautiful, or terrible his fantasies might be, Tamburlaine proceeds to act them out. He first—indeed, he always—imagines what it might be most glorious, or exciting, or terrible to do, and then he does it. To give one obvious example, Tamburlaine hears someone tell Cosroe, the new King of Persia, that he will shortly have his wish, and 'ride in triumph through Persepolis'. This idea captures Tamburlaine's imagination, and so he makes the wish (and the phrase) his own:

> And ride in triumph through Persepolis!
> Is it not brave to be a king, Techelles,
> Usumcasane and Theridamas?
> Is it not passing brave to be a king,
> And ride in triumph through Persepolis?   (II. v. 50–4)

He instantly vows to have the triumphal ride for himself; then he proceeds to fulfil that vow. Furthermore, Tamburlaine's desires are got with full content. He exults in winning: in love, in power, and in war.

Thus Tamburlaine's dreams—whether they be innocently white, dangerously red, or deadly black—will be acted out; and woe to those whose lives stand in the level of those dreams. For Tamburlaine is representative of all our mighty conquerors, or, if one prefers Milton's terms for them, those destroyers and plagues of men, who, at whatever cost to others, have had their rides through Persepolis, and who, more recently, have had their faces outlined in the sky by aircraft. Like Tamburlaine, these historical 'supermen' have appealed to the imagination of others, partly because they have so ruthlessly, so audaciously, dared to be what they wanted to be, to take what they wanted to have, to do what they wanted to do; partly, also, because they dared to do what others might like to do, if only they could, and because they afforded devoted followers the privilege of acting out fantasies of their own.[9] Also, surely, our conquerors have been admired because they achieved, on earth, a correspondence between the individual will to power and the possession of great power. Indeed, throughout his play about the ambitious Scythian shepherd who, 'by his rare and wonderful conquests', became a 'most puissant and mighty monarch'; whose customs were as peremptory as 'wrathful planets, death, or destiny'; and who, for his tyranny and terror in war, was termed 'The Scourge of God', Marlowe effectively reminds us of the historical fact that the human dream of power, if it is unchecked by limits on the individual capacity to act out that dream, is itself as attractive, as potent, as awesome, as terrible, as deadly a force of nature, as Tamburlaine.

On the other hand, the dream of power may end in a nightmare of impotence, and Marlowe knew that too. His tragic Dr. Faustus, who once imagined he might be like a mighty god, could be 'divine' only 'in show'. Unlike Tamburlaine's, Faustus's dreams of power and glory never correspond to the facts. Indeed, the last dream of beauty, for which he forfeited his soul in that fatal kiss, never had the true, substantial body of Helen of Troy.[10]

Yet the spirits that attend on Dr. Faustus, like certain private devils of our own, have the power to assume some very pleasing shapes. Thus one might well sympathize with Faustus's rejection of prosaic reality in favour of the charming delights of the imagination. For how could his vision of reality, in the form of an ugly Old Man, compete with an illusion that was so fair:

> O, thou art fairer than the evening's air,
> Clad in the beauty of a thousand stars.
> Brighter art thou than flaming Jupiter,

[9] See John Fowles, *The Magus* (London, 1972), p. 367: 'One of the great fallacies of our time is that the Nazis rose to power because they imposed order on chaos. Precisely the opposite is true—they were successful because they imposed chaos on order. They tore up the commandments, they denied the superego, what you will. They said, "You may persecute the minority, you may kill, you may torture, you may couple and breed without love." They offered humanity all its great temptations.'

[10] See W. W. Greg, 'The Damnation of Faustus', *MLR* 41 (1946), 97–107. See also Helen Gardner, 'Milton's "Satan" and the Theme of Damnation in Elizabethan Tragedy', *Essays and Studies* (1948), pp. 36–66, reprinted in her *Reading of 'Paradise Lost'*. My discussion of *Dr. Faustus* and *Macbeth* is also indebted to a lecture on *Macbeth* which Dame Helen delivered at Oxford, in the autumn of 1973.

> When he appear'd to hapless Semele:
> More lovely than the monarch of the sky,
> In wanton Arethusa's azur'd arms,
> And none but thou shalt be my paramour.   (v. i. 110–16)

Yet the tendency of the human imagination to build its own castles 'in the air' (IV. vi. 2) can lead to a substitution of 'idle fantasies' for genuine accomplishment. It does, in effect, wither 'Apollo's laurel bough', the intellectual aspiration, which sometime grew within this learned man:

Faustus.   What means this show? Speak, Mephostophilis.
Mephostophilis.   Nothing, Faustus, but to delight thy mind.   (II. i. 83–4)

Belzebub.   Faustus, we are come from hell in person to show thee some pastime. Sit down and thou shalt behold the Seven Deadly Sins appear to thee in their own proper shapes and likenesses.
Faustus.   That sight will be as pleasant to me as Paradise was to Adam the first day of his creation.
Lucifer.   Talk not of Paradise or Creation, but mark the show.
                                                                (II. ii. 102–8)

The show itself is trivial, grotesque. But 'O how this sight doth delight my soul', says Faustus, who is rapidly becoming addicted to illusions, and so losing his soul, his divine intelligence, his rational powers to them.

The reliance upon illusions of one form or another can indeed take the form of an addiction; it can become habitual. As the Spanish proverb says, 'Habits are at first cobwebs, then cables'. And in the B-text of the tragedy, the Old Man issues an explicit warning about the force of habit:

> O gentle Faustus, leave this damned art,
> This magic, that will charm thy soul to hell,
> . . . .
> Yet, yet, thou hast an amiable soul,
> *If sin by custom grow not into nature.*
>   (v. i. 36–42, *emphasis mine*)

But to alter 'custom' requires decisive action. To change a habit requires total withdrawal from it, a reversal of the habitual behaviour. 'Assume a virtue, if you have it not', Hamlet tells Gertrude, for

> That monster, custom, who all sense doth eat,
> Of habits devil, is angel yet in this,
> That to the use of actions fair and good
> He likewise gives a frock of livery,
> That aptly is put on. Refrain to-night,
> And that shall lend a kind of easiness
> To the next abstinence: the next more easy;
> *For use almost can change the stamp of nature,*
> And either [master] the devil, or throw him out
> With wondrous potency.   (III. iv. 160–70—*emphasis mine*)

Individual human beings can, by altering their behaviour, master the devils without and throw out the devils within. By sustaining certain patterns of behaviour, they can alter their own nature for the better, just as they can, by sustaining other patterns of behaviour, alter their own nature for the worse.[11] Once made, his contract with Lucifer must continually be reaffirmed (II. ii. 90–101); and so Faustus consistently acts upon the promptings of Mephostophilis. There are times when he wants to repent, but he cannot reverse the course of his behaviour and thus act upon a decision to do so.

He can, however, almost too easily imagine the alternative of repentance, just as he can, all too easily, imagine the alternative of damnation:

> What art thou, Faustus, but a man condemn'd to die?
> Thy fatal time draws to a final end.
> Despair doth drive distrust into my thoughts;
> Confound these passions with a quiet sleep.
> Tush, Christ did call the thief upon the cross,
> Then rest thee, Faustus, quiet in conceit.   (IV. iv. 18–21)

Faustus thus struggles back and forth, to the very end, between an imaginative conception of himself whereby he retains the freedom to repent and the opposite conception of himself whereby he cannot repent:

---

[11] See Bettelheim, *The Informed Heart*, p. 25. 'Only dimly at first, but with ever greater clarity, did I . . . come to see that soon how a man acts can alter what he is. Those who stood up well in the camps became better men, those who acted badly soon became bad men; and this, or at least so it seemed, independent of their past life history and their former personality make-up.' Of course the force of habitual behaviour has been noted ever since Aristotle, and he was probably not the first to notice it.

Faustus. . . . I will renounce this magic and repent.
Good Angel. Faustus, repent; yet God will pity thee.
Bad Angel. Thou art a spirit; God cannot pity thee.
Faustus. Who buzzeth in mine ears I am a spirit?
   Be I a devil, yet God may pity me;
   Yes, God will pity me if I repent.
Bad Angel. Ay, but Faustus never shall repent.
Faustus. My heart's so harden'd I cannot repent.   (II. ii. 11–18)

In the end, Faustus looks up and sees Christ's blood stream for him in the firmament, but then he sees Lucifer. And the upper stage may be bare at the time he sees both visions.

When he says goodbye to the scholars, Faustus believes that he is physically controlled by Lucifer and Mephostophilis, but the scholars see nothing there; they see nothing at all, which, in this particular instance, may indeed be all there is to see:

Faustus. . . . Ah my God—I would weep, but the devil draws in
   my tears. . . . O, he stays my tongue. I would lift up my hands,
   but see, they hold them, they hold them.
All. Who, Faustus?[12]   (v. ii. 51–4)

Possibly nothing holds Faustus, nothing pulls him down, except his own imagination, his own conception of himself; and that imagination, that conception which was acted out for twenty-four years, was what finally claimed him, at last, for Lucifer. So Faustus finally becomes the tragic victim of those very forces which he himself so boldly sought to summon and command; he is, quite literally, torn apart by his own illusions.

The mind's its own place, and will seek out its own heavens and hells:

Faustus. When I behold the heavens then I repent,
   And curse thee, wicked Mephostophilis,
   Because thou hast depriv'd me of those joys.
Mephostophilis. 'Twas thine own seeking, Faustus, thank thyself.
    (II. ii. 1–4)

Furthermore, it may create its own gods, and, indeed, deify its own desires:

---

[12] It seems interesting, here, to contrast the devils who appear only to Faustus with the Ghost who appears to the soldiers and Horatio, as well as to Hamlet.

Faustus. 'Abjure this magic, turn to God again.'
Ay, and Faustus will turn to God again.
To God? He loves thee not.
The God thou serv'st is thine own appetite.   (ii. i. 8–11)

In so far as Faustus was free to choose, he made his own hell: *Quisque suos patimur manes.* And, after all, we have the word of Mephostophilis himself that the pains of hell are only 'as great as have the human souls of men'. Hell is, from one point of view, a state of mind. It may be produced by illusions and superstitious fears, with no more reality than Elysium. Yet Marlowe's God and Lucifer alike seem to represent figments of man's imagination grown so powerful that they finally have become realities, in that they can wield tyrannical power over the very minds and imaginations that invested them with all their powers to begin with. Real heroes and deluded fools alike have, as heretics, been burned alive by their power. Yet for all we know, neither heaven or hell may have any existence at all, *except* as states of mind; and the traditional means to bring people to superhuman glory in some afterlife may, as the Bad Angel said they were, be themselves 'illusions' that 'make men foolish that do use them most'. This possibility certainly exists, and Marlowe boldly takes it into account. For that matter, Heaven itself, or so says Mephostophilis (who ought to know, since he was born there), is 'not half so fair' as 'any man that breathes on earth' (ii. ii. 6–7).

From the moment he makes his contract with Lucifer, Faustus is indeed rather like a disembodied 'spirit'—he loses touch with the men that breathe on earth. In the beginning, he had any number of intellectual pursuits available to him, and any one of them might have positively benefited other men. There was law, medicine, and logic. But of course Faustus rejects the human for the superhuman, and proceeds to reduce his many alternatives to two: divinity and necromancy. Indeed, it seems that the human brain has a pronounced tendency to reduce any number of choices to two: this is why 'either–or' commands like 'Take up the sword again, or take up me' are so effective, even when they pose false alternatives—Lady Anne could have put down that sword and still refused Richard. Once one such alternative has been chosen, however, it is hard to go back on the choice. Once Faustus has chosen necromancy, and acted on his choice, he has only two alternatives left: be resolute or repent. This narrowing down of possibilities no doubt reflects genuine processes of human psychology, behaviour, and experience. Yet since alternatives of this kind are frequently fallacious ('he who is not for us is against us'), one should beware of getting trapped by them. Certainly Faustus is tragically trapped in a cosmic deadlock. He can go back, or he can go forward; either alternative represents a taking of the easiest way out, on the one hand, and a terrible threat, on the other.[13]

Marlowe's lords of heaven and hell are identical in their hostile opposition to human freedom of thought. So far as intellectual states of mind are concerned, both God and Lucifer rule police states. Thus, when the devils from hell impose one set of restrictions upon Faustus's liberty to read and think, their tyranny seems simply a photo-negative reversal of the Good Angel's original set of prohibitions and threats. Here are the parallel passages.

> *Good Angel.* O Faustus, lay that damned book aside,
>   And gaze not on it lest it tempt thy soul,
>   And heap God's heavy wrath upon thy head.
>   Read, read the scriptures: that is blasphemy.   (I. i. 68–71)

> *Belzebub.* We are come to tell thee thou dost injure us.
> *Lucifer.* Thou call'st on Christ contrary to thy promise.
> *Belzebub.* Thou should'st not think on God.
> *Lucifer.* Think on the devil.
>
>   . . . .
> *Faustus.*   . . . Pardon me in this,
>   And Faustus vows never to look to heaven,
>   Never to name God or to pray to him,
>   To burn his scriptures, slay his ministers,
>   And make my spirits pull his churches down.   (II. ii. 90–9)

Since they are equally merciless to heretics, God and Lucifer join together, in the end, to replace Faustus's brief vision of Christ's mercy with images of their pitiless wrath:

> See, see, where Christ's blood streams in the firmament!
> One drop would save my soul, half a drop. Ah, my Christ!
> Rend not my heart for naming of my Christ!
> Yet will I call on him. O spare me, Lucifer!
> Where is it now? 'Tis gone:
> And see where God stretcheth out his arm,

[13] I am here indebted to a paper by Jim Morgan, written when he was a student at Vassar in 1973.

And bends his ireful brows.
Mountains and hills, come, come, and fall on me,
And hide me from the heavy wrath of God.
. . . .
My God, my God! Look not so fierce on me.
Adders and serpents, let me breathe awhile.
Ugly hell, gape not! Come not, Lucifer!
I'll burn my books.   (v. ii. 139–47, 181–4)

Since neither God nor the Devil will tolerate intellectual liberty, it is difficult to decide to whom Faustus directs his final promise to burn his books, or to decide to which of those books Faustus refers. Have God and Lucifer so combined to damn him, by the end of his tragedy, that it does not matter? 'Whither should I fly', he asks, 'If unto God, he'll throw me down to hell' (ii. i. 77–8).

In writing *Dr. Faustus*, Marlowe insists upon his own freedom to criticize the ways of gods as well as the ways of men; for even as he criticizes his deluded hero, he boldly criticizes the tyrannies of both heaven and hell. He thus makes it difficult for his audience simply to take Heaven's side against Faustus, or to take Faustus's side against Hell, or to take Hell's side against Heaven. And through these deadlocks he implies that we ourselves remain at liberty to make up our own minds about the alternatives faced by his most exceptional Everymen, to choose our own gods and our own destinies. We are even free to scorn, as Marlowe himself was said to have done, all 'bugbeares' and 'hobgoblins', and so to reject any and all tyrannically restricted conceptions of man's essentially protean nature.

That intellectual vision which Marlowe's damned hero had once hoped to extend 'as far as doth the mind of man' remains man's glory: 'No man', says Donne, 'doth refine and exalt Nature to the heighth it would beare.' The human imagination that, acted upon, has created hells on earth has also created visions of a better world and so improved the real one. And transcendently unselfish dreams have also been acted out by men. 'In short, a man is as good as his fantasies', writes Doris Lessing, who has 'no time for people who haven't experimented with themselves, deliberately tried the frontiers'.[14] Indeed the Faustian desire to 'try the utmost'

14 Doris Lessing, *The Golden Notebook*, p. 464. On p. 554, she argues that 'There's only one real sin, and that is to persuade oneself that the second-best is anything but the second-best'. Faustus's sin against the Holy Ghost may have been his failure to accomplish, in twenty-four years of life, what he might have accomplished—a sin of

may very well characterize the best human beings as well as the worst. Certainly, in spite of all the pressures in favour of conformity, in spite of the shackles of dogma, orthodoxy, and superstitious fear which have been imposed upon their behaviour and imagination and intellect, our greatest liberators, along with our worst tyrants, have found that there was 'no contentment but in proceeding'.

Of course Marlowe's play very obviously insists upon the potentially tragic nature of human freedom. Therein lies one of its claims to greatness, its bitter grandeur. Yet it also affirms precisely that freedom to choose how they will think and behave which dignifies human beings over all other animals. 'The brutes', says Pico della Mirandola, bring with them 'from their mother's womb' all that they will ever possess. But God bestowed upon man 'seeds pregnant with all possibilities'. Whichever of these a man shall cultivate will mature and bear fruit in him. So Pico's God informs his Adam.

We have given you, Oh Adam, no visage proper to yourself, nor any endowment properly your own, in order that whatever place, whatever form, whatever gifts you may, with premeditation, select, these same you may have and possess though your own judgment and decision. The nature of all other creatures is defined and restricted within laws which We have laid down; you, by contrast, impeded by no such restrictions, may, by your own free will, to whose custody we have assigned you, trace for yourself the lineaments of your own nature. . . . We have made you . . . in order that you may, as the free and proud shaper of your own being, fashion yourself in the form you may prefer.[15]

A physical anthropologist has, more recently, made several related points about our condition:

'The conviction of wisdom', wrote Montaigne . . . 'is the plague of man'. . . . In one period we believe ourselves governed by immutable laws; in the next, by chance. In one period angels hover over our birth; in the following time we are planetary waifs, the product of a meaningless and ever altering chemistry. We exchange halos in one era for fangs in another. Our religious and philosophical conceptions

---

which the man who wrote *Tamburlaine*, *Dr. Faustus*, *Edward the Second*, *The Jew of Malta*, etc., before he died at twenty-nine, was clearly not guilty.

[15] Giovanni Pico della Mirandola, *Oration on the Dignity of Man*, trans. Robert A. Caponigri (Chicago, 1956), pp. 7–8.

change so rapidly that the [convictions] . . . for which millions yielded up their lives produce only bored yawns in a later generation. . . .

Few of us can be saints; few of us are total monsters. To the degree that we let others project upon us erroneous or unbalanced conceptions of our natures, we may unconsciously reshape our own image to less pleasing forms. It is one thing to be 'realistic', as many are fond of saying, about human nature. It is another thing entirely to let that consideration set limits to our spiritual aspirations or to precipitate us into cynicism and despair. We are protean in many things, and stand between extremes.[16]

Several of these insights are very dramatically illustrated by Shakespeare as well as by Marlowe. Like Marlowe's heroes, Macbeth chooses his own destiny. Like Faustus, he creates his own hell within and round about him. In watching *Macbeth*, one watches custom change the stamp of nature, sees habit grown into nature itself as he reshapes his own image before our very eyes. Yet it is only through a deliberate effort of will that Macbeth can suppress all kindness, and act out his most 'black and deep' desires; and the forces which operate on Macbeth and Faustus alike do not operate entirely from within. Faustus's devils were hovering around, just waiting to be summoned; and he was encouraged to conjure by the earthly influences of Valdes and Cornelius. Macbeth's witches appear from nowhere to infect his imagination with horrid images of murder; then his wife provides the spur which pricks the side of his intent to kill the King. Indeed, given the genius of a Shakespeare, it is possible to re-create that subtle interplay between the external environment and the individual human being, between the past, the present, and the future, which makes up the substance of human life. Macbeth's tragedy, like Hamlet's, involves this interplay. Forces from the outside, influences from the environment, the witches of the future may suggest potentialities that lie latent within the individual. They may suggest actions to him, they may even come together to destroy him; but they cannot force the mind to respond positively to their influences.

Milton puts it thus:

> Evil into the mind of God or Man
> May come and go, so unapprov'd, and leave

16 Loren Eiseley, *The Unexpected Universe* (Harmondsworth, 1973), 142–4.

> No spot or blame behind: Which gives me hope
> That what in sleep thou didst abhor to dream,
> Waking thou never wilt consent to do.[17]

Likewise, good influences may be rejected. The human brain thus can censor its own operations: it may approve of, criticize, or dismiss external influences, just as it can approve of, criticize, or reject its own productions. Banquo's imagination appears to have been comparatively immune to any serious infection from the witches; and of course Macbeth himself was initially appalled by his own 'horrible imaginings'.

Yet if they are imaginatively dwelt upon, even those thoughts of evil which most repel can, in time, become natural. Or so goes Sin's own, original, first-hand description of the progression of responses that she tends to elicit:

> back they recoil'd afraid
> At first, and call'd me *Sin*, and for a Sign
> Portentous held me; but familiar grown,
> I pleas'd.   (*Paradise Lost*, II. 759–62)

In his *Essay on Man*, Pope concurs with her:

> Vice is a monster of so frightful mien,
> As to be hated needs but to be seen;
> Yet seen too oft, familiar with her face,
> We first endure, then pity, then embrace.

So does Middleton in his *Women Beware Women*:

> Sin tastes at the first draught like wormwood-water,
> But drunk again, 'tis nectar ever after.

Indeed, he dramatically illustrates this process in *The Changeling*. In that play, the beautiful virgin, Beatrice-Joanna, is initially

---

[17] *Paradise Lost*, V. 117–21. This seems to have proved true, so far as Bettelheim was concerned, in the concentration camps. See *The Informed Heart*, p. 25: 'The way a person acted in a showdown could not be deduced from his inner, hidden motives which, likely as not, were conflicting. Neither his heroic nor his cowardly dreams, his free associations or conscious fantasies permitted correct predictions as to whether, in the next moment, he would risk his life to protect the life of others, or out of panic betray many in a vain effort to gain some advantage for himself.' Experience 'with both analysed and unanalysed persons in the camps' convinced Bettelheim that 'when the chips were down it was utterly unimportant why a person acted the way he did; the only thing that counted was how he acted'. King Claudius, at prayer, fears judgement above, for 'there the action lies/In his true nature' (*Hamlet*, III. iii. 60–1). In the last analysis, we may all have to judge ourselves, not on the basis of what we wanted to do, or why we did what we did, but solely on the basis of what we did.

disgusted by the very sight of the ugly villain, De Flores. Later
she makes him her partner in murder, though she is subsequently
horrified when he insists that she pay for his services with her
virginity. De Flores, however, is absolutely certain that she will
'come to love anon' what she now fears and faints to think upon.
He soon becomes indispensable to her; they continue their affair
and die together. Beatrice-Joanna's vision of evil was, both
allegorically and literally, first abhorred, then suffered, and finally
embraced: familiar grown, De Flores pleased.

So the first devil that Faustus summons seems a monster of a
frightful mien, but the last one appears gorgeous. And thus,
though the very imagination of his first murder makes Macbeth's
seated heart knock at his ribs against the use of nature,

> My thought, whose murder yet is but fantastical,
> Shakes so my single state of man that function
> Is smother'd in surmise, and nothing is
> But what is not.   (I. iii. 138–42)

by the end of his tragedy, direness, which has become familiar to
his slaughterous thoughts, cannot even cause him to start.

At the beginning, his wife accuses him of cowardice:

> Art thou afeard
> To be the same in thine own act and valour
> As thou art in desire?   (I. vii. 39–41)

Unlike Tamburlaine, Macbeth is unable, at the outset, to act out
instantly, without hesitation or internal conflict, his any and every
desire. But he tries, indeed he forces himself, to learn to do so;
and before the end of the play he does learn. The process operates
as follows.

'Things bad begun', he says, 'make strong themselves by ill'
(III. ii. 55), so perhaps sheer perseverance in murder may give him
strength for more murders. But even after the murder of Banquo,
Macbeth experiences the 'initiate fear that wants hard use'. So far
as murder is concerned, he and his wife are 'yet but young in deed'.
'Strange things I have in head, that will to hand', he tells her,
'Which must be acted ere they may be scann'd' (III. iv. 139–44).
Then, after his final encounter with the witches, he vows that

> from this moment
> The very firstlings of my heart shall be

The firstlings of my hand. And even now,
To crown my thoughts with acts, be it thought and done.

(IV. i. 146–9)

Even as he moves forward, 'in blood so deep' that going back
were as tedious as proceeding, he grows accustomed to slaughterous thoughts and deeds alike:

> The time has been, my senses would have cool'd
> To hear a night-shriek; and my fell of hair
> Would at a dismal treatise rouse and stir
> As life were in 't: I have supp'd full with horrors;
> Direness, familiar to my slaughterous thoughts,
> Cannot once start me.   (V. v. 10–15)

Through a conscious effort of the will, he forms the habit of
acting out his most terrible fantasies; while, for Macbeth and his
wife alike, the substance of their ambition itself becomes a kind of
horrible shadow, a hideous dream. For though they do indeed win
what they once wanted, they lose everything they once had. All
their desires are got without content:

> . . . let the frame of things disjoint, both the worlds suffer,
> Ere we will eat our meal in fear and sleep
> In the affliction of these terrible dreams
> That shake us nightly: better be with the dead,
> Whom we, to gain our peace, have sent to peace,
> Than on the torture of the mind to lie
> In restless ecstasy.   (III. ii. 16–22)

Survival, life, is no victory for them; death is no punishment.
Death would be preferable: 'Had I but died an hour before this
chance', says Macbeth, in his definitive statement about life's
battles lost, 'I had lived a blessed time.' Like Claudius, Macbeth
feels his secret murders sticking on his head, so his memory and
imagination are haunted by ghosts. Though she once scorned
memory and imagination alike, and feared no painted devils, Lady
Macbeth is finally destroyed by her 'thick-coming fancies', by her
'rooted sorrow', by the 'written troubles' of her brain (v. iii.
38–42). 'What's done is done', she once said; but who, she now
asks, would have thought the gracious old man, who had resembled
her father as he slept, to have had so much blood in him?

Lady Macbeth, however, once mocked the 'air-drawn dagger'
which Macbeth said led him to Duncan, and her mockery, in that

instance, may have had a valid point. The fatal vision which hung before Macbeth's hand may indeed have been 'a false creation' proceeding from his 'heat-oppressed brain', which had no power except what was lent to it by his own mind. The danger to Macbeth, like the danger to Faustus, lay not so much in what he was, but in what his own imagination chose to fasten upon, in his own vision of himself. Scotland's hero, who had the golden opinions of 'all sorts of people' when his tragedy began, determined to act the part of a villain, and, poor player, he finally becomes a 'bloodier villain' than 'terms can give him out'.

Macbeth 'filed his mind', defiled his imagination, and then 'bent up each corporeal agent' to conform to his distorted vision of himself, and he is thus slowly transformed into something very different from his original self. Here, as in *The Changeling* and *Paradise Lost*, as sin grows familiar, and thus less hideous to him, the sinner, once bright, becomes a kind of monster, a changeling.

The freedoms to choose our own conceptions of ourselves, to act on those conceptions, and thus, perhaps, become what we have conceived ourselves to be, may indeed thrust inescapable temptations on all of us:

> Oftentimes, to win us to our harm,
> The instruments of darkness tell us truths,
> Win us with honest trifles, to betray's
> In deepest consequence. (I. iii. 122–6)

Like Macbeth, one may be tempted with seeming realities about oneself until these realities take shape in the mind and impose themselves on one's own nature, one's own future. But the instruments of darkness can only open a way and wait for mortal nobility or depravity to take its course. Macbeth was literally tricked into tragedy by equivocal prophecies about his future. Under their spell, he forfeits the future that he might have had had he not acted on them, and he always looks back on that forfeited future with bitter regret:

> And that which should accompany old age,
> As honour, love, obedience, troops of friends,
> I must not look to have; but, in their stead,
> Curses, not loud but deep, mouth-honour, breath,
> Which the poor heart would fain deny, and dare not.
> (V. iii. 24–8)

To the very end, Macbeth's tragedy is compounded of anticipations and memories, desires and regrets. 'The future is not,' wrote Kierkegaard: 'It borrows its strength from the man itself, and when it has tricked him out of this, then it appears outside of him as the enemy he must meet'. So Birnam Forest comes to Dunsinane, and Macbeth encounters an adversary who was not of woman born:

> And be these juggling fiends no more believed,
> That palter with us in a double sense;
> That keep the word of promise to our ear,
> And break it to our hope.   (v. viii. 19–22)

Like Faustus, Macbeth is the victim of terrible tricksters. A fiendish sneer, a demonic '''twas thine own choosing'; a triumphant, contemptuous, sardonic, 'sorry about that', 'too bad about you'; a last, cackling, laugh—these seem the only, and, perhaps, the proper, cosmic responses to their final agonies. The human responses, however, must be genuine pity and terror.

'Can the devil speak true?' Of course he can, if we believe what he says, and so make it come true. It may well be that, by way of his juggling fiends, Shakespeare passes on to us 'the deadliest message' to be encountered in 'all of literature': 'what we wish will come'.[18]

Thus Shakespeare's poetry itself palters with us in a double sense. He is out to deceive us with his dramatic illusions, with his very own instruments of darkness, and, simultaneously, to tell us truths that may set us free from some far more dangerous illusions than those of the theatre. This fact creates another series of critical problems.

[18] See Loren Eiseley's discussion of *Macbeth*, 'Instruments of Darkness', in *The Night Country* (New York, 1971), pp. 47–55.

V 'Stay, illusion!':
Some poetic godgames

> Thus, neither of us is alive when the reader opens this
> book. But while the blood still throbs through my writing
> hand, you are still as much part of blessed matter as I am,
> and I can still talk to you from here to Alaska. . . . And
> do not pity C. Q. One had to choose between him and
> H. H., and one wanted H. H. to exist at least a couple of
> months longer, so as to have him make you live in the
> minds of later generations. I am thinking of aurochs and
> angels, the secret of durable pigments, prophetic sonnets,
> the refuge of art. And this is the only immortality you and
> I may share, my Lolita.   VLADIMIR NABOKOV

> Couldst thou make men to live eternally,
> Or being dead, raise them to life again,
> Then this profession were to be esteem'd.
>   MARLOWE, *Dr. Faustus*

CENTURIES ago, while the blood still throbbed in their writing
hands, the poets discussed here felt compelled to make people they
knew, or beings they only imagined, live in the minds of later
generations. And indeed they can still deceive us into feeling that
some of their creations are, or were, or might have been, as much
a part of 'blessed matter' as they themselves were, as we ourselves
are. To make their specially favoured characters spring to life in
our minds, and live on in our memories, seems, for them, to have
taken priority over all else: even over any appeals to our moral
judgement. Thus, their more remarkable, richly conceived characters, whether they embody virtue or vice, will dominate the
imagination; while those more ordinary creations, who serve such
characters as foils, or as members of their supporting cast, will,
whatever their virtues, engage us less. That most 'wonderful
piece of work', the Cleopatra whom only Shakespeare could have
created, cannot but win out over poor Octavia, who, by comparison, seems dull and ordinary in all her ways. Octavia is a very

good woman, but she was deliberately made to be a routinely good one. There are good women, very like Octavia, all around in the drama of the period. There is no other Cleopatra.

Even though profoundly moral messages may be communicated through many of their works, the process of creating such characters as Cleopatra, Falstaff, Richard III, the Wife of Bath, the Pardoner, Eve and Satan goes beyond morality. It seems to be the human counterpart to the non-human process that shaped cats and cobras, peacocks and starlings, tigers and lambs, the real Octavia, the first Cleopatra, the original Tamburlaine, and which, to justify its ways to man, once justified its creations purely *as* creations, in mighty lines of poetry, like these:

> Behold now Behemoth, which I made with thee;
> He eateth grass as an ox.
> Lo now, his strength is in his loins,
> And his force is in the muscles of his belly.
> He moveth his tail like a cedar:
> The sinews of his thighs are knit together.
> His bones are as tubes of brass;
> His limbs are like bars of iron.
> He is the chief of the ways of God:
> He only that made him can make his sword to approach unto him.

Likewise, the poets who made them can, if they wish, play with their Leviathans as with a bird. They can point the way to the dwelling of light, and, as for darkness, they can show where is the place thereof. Then, in the end, they may whisper to us, of their chief creations, 'Hitherto shalt thou come, but no further'; 'he only that made him can make his sword to approach unto him'.

'For the Lord in the whirlwind', says Isak Dinesen, 'pleads the defense of the artist, and of the artist only':

He blows up the moral scruples and the moral sufferings of his public; he does not attempt to justify his show by any argument on right and wrong. . . . Yes, he speaks about the horrors and abominations of existence, and airily asks his public if they, too, will play with them as with a bird, and let their young persons do the same.[1]

[1] 'A Consolatory Tale', *Winter's Tales* (New York, 1942), p. 294. See also Leonardo da Vinci, as quoted by E. H. Gombrich in *Art and Illusion*, p. 81. For Leonardo, the painter is 'the Lord of all manner of people and of all things'. If he wishes 'to see beauties to fall in love with, it is in his power to bring them forth, and if he wants to see monstrous things that frighten or are foolish or laughable or indeed to be pitied, he is their Lord and God.'

The amoral force of the creative process itself seems far too obvious to be denied or discounted by any amount of criticism. Too many writers have insisted upon the way their own creative energies may associate themselves with forms of human and natural energy, and do so quite independently of any moral judgement. Shakespeare, says Coleridge, 'had read nature too heedfully not to know that courage, intellect, and strength of character were the most impressive forms of power, and that to power in itself, without reference to any moral end, an inevitable admiration and complacency appertains, whether it be displayed in the conquests of a Napoleon or Tamberlane, or in the foam and thunder of a cataract'.[2] Indeed, Keats's classic account of the 'negative capability' of the poet describes a capability which he shared with the masters of poetry he so much admired, and with modern novelists as well: 'The point is,' writes Doris Lessing, 'and it is the point that obsesses me . . . once I say that words like good/bad, strong/weak, are irrelevant, I am accepting amorality, and I do accept it the moment I start to write "a story", a "novel", because I simply don't care. All I care about is that I should describe Willi and Maryrose so that a reader can feel their reality.'[3]

In fact, his amoral, creative energy is likely to keep the writer closer to the truth of things as they are than any number of moral convictions concerning things as they ought to be. Or, in Proust's terms, artists must think not of their own predilections, 'but of a truth which does not ask our preferences and forbids us to give them a thought'. The writer will succeed as an artist only on condition that 'when he is studying the laws of Art, making his experiments and his discoveries, as delicate as those of Science, he thinks of nothing . . . except the truth that is before him'.[4]

In *Paradise Lost* Milton describes his sinners so that his readers can feel the reality of his Satan, his Eve, and thus recognize the truths about human experience displayed in them. This is one reason why C. S. Lewis's analysis of the successive sins that Eve falls into seems more concerned with the reader's morals than with Milton's meaning, with what Sidney would call his 'passionate

[2] *Coleridge's Shakespearean Criticism*, ed. T. M. Raysor, vol. I (London, 1930), p. 58.
[3] Doris Lessing, *The Golden Notebook*, p. 67.
[4] Marcel Proust, *The Past Recaptured*, trans. Frederick A. Blosson (New York, 1932), pp. 1008, 1120. Subsequent quotations from Proust are from this edition of *Remembrance of Things Past*. The other books referred to were translated by C. K. Scott Moncrieff.

describing of passions'. Lewis, in writing about Milton, succeeds
primarily as a moralist, whereas Milton's success is that of an
artist. Lewis presents the abstractions and exaggerations of the
moralist in place of Milton's living picture of his own Eve's
'excitement, elation, momentary desire for separateness and
superiority, immediate realization of the peril she has incurred,
with the hateful thought of Adam living on without her, happy
with "another Eve", and final resolution, in which she seems to
express the truth of her own nature'. For that matter, it is not
enough to demonstrate by moral arguments that 'the Devil is an
Ass' when the common reader 'so obstinately persists in regarding
him as heroic'.[5]

Of course moral convictions may coexist with amoral, creative
energy; indeed, they may complement each other. An essentially
moral poet may criticize the behaviour of his own immoral creations even as he may, with all the force of his creative energy,
boldly question his own judgements, defiantly challenge his own,
most deeply held, principles, and so contain his own contra-
dictions. A quick look at some obvious forms of creative delight
and moral instruction that manifest themselves in Jonson's
Volpone can illustrate several ways in which moral and amoral
energies may sometimes clash, sometimes co-operate, within an
individual work.

Until some very rude awakenings occur, practically everybody
in the play lives in a golden dream of anticipation. Volpone himself keeps ordering banquets and anticipating orgies of delight
that somehow never arrive. He boasts to Celia that he feeds others
'in expectation', but so he also feeds himself:

> my dwarf shall dance,
> My eunuch sing, my fool make up the antic
> Whil'st we, in changed shapes, act Ovid's tales,
> Thou, like Europa now, and I like Jove,
> Then I like Mars and thou like Erycine,
> So, of the rest, till we have quite run through
> And wearied all the fables of the gods.
> Then will I have thee in more modern forms,
> Attired like some sprightly dame of France,
> Brave Tuscan lady, or proud Spanish beauty;
> Sometimes unto the Persian Sophie's wife;

[5] Quotations are from Helen Gardner, *A Reading of 'Paradise Lost'*, pp. ix, 14–15.

Or the Grand Signior's mistress; and for change,
To one of our most artful courtesans,
Or some quick Negro, or cold Russian.   (III. vii. 219–32)

Of course Celia's refusal to play her part, or rather, her parts, in his erotic masquerades denies Volpone the delights of re-enacting all the antics of the gods. And then the entrance of Bonario deprives him of even the brutish satisfactions of rape.

Nevertheless, Volpone's lines retain their own wild and peculiar power:

Thy baths shall be the juice of July-flowers,
Spirit of roses, and of violets,
The milk of unicorns and panther's breath
Gather'd in bags and mix'd with Cretan wines.
Our drink shall be prepared gold and amber.   (III. vii. 213–17)

Volpone's imagination roves the world and its myths, commandeering them with a privateer's bravura, making all the glittering spoils his own. 'Then will I *have* thee.' 'None but thou shalt be *my* paramour.' Volpone and Faustus both want to grasp, to seize, to possess, to summon and command their visions of delight in the forms they most desire. They are thus the dramatic and dialectical opposites of those characters, like Celia or the Old Man, whose sense of morality bids them shun such fabulous fantasies, such sensual delights:

Celia. Good sir, these things might move a mind affected
     With such delights; but I . . .
     Cannot be taken with these sensual baits.   (III. vii. 206–10)

Celia's imagination cannot be captured by Volpone's fantastic lines. Yet Volpone's imagination seems notably comparable to that of his creator, who, whether his vision be of beauty or evil or folly, will set out to capture, to shape and to hold that vision, and so pass it on to others: 'Phant'sie, I tell you, has dreams that have wings,/And dreams that have honey, and dreams that have stings.' 'Stay, illusion!' is the order that the poet may issue unto any number of beautiful, delightful, disturbing, and terrible apparitions: to honest ghosts and juggling fiends; to Comus and Sabrina; to Caliban and Ariel; to the Fox and the Swan; and even unto God and Lucifer themselves.

So Jonson summons up characters who will act out his own fantasies, embody his own visions. He thus re-creates Volpone's erotic fantasies, and, for that matter, Sir Politic's idiotic schemes, with all the creative energy at his disposal, in order to display before us a unique vision of human greed and gullibility:

Even the human beings most stupid as to gestures, remarks and spontaneously expressed sentiments demonstrate laws that they are not aware of but which the artist unexpectedly discovers in them. Because of his studies of this type, the common herd considers the writer unkind, but without justification because in a ridiculous trait the artist sees a splendid generality.[6]

Jonson, in this sense, at least, is not unkind to his knaves and fools—far from it. In them he finds his own sources of inspiration. In them he discovers laws of human nature that they themselves may not be aware of, and which his own audience, but for him, might not have noticed. For instance, there is the psychological law whereby his characters will refuse to admit evidence contrary to their own wishes:

> Each of 'em
> Is so possess'd and stuff'd with his own hopes,
> That anything unto the contrary,
> Never so true, or never so apparent,
> Never so palpable, they will resist it— (v. ii. 23–7)

There is the law whereby they will consistently underestimate the knavery of others. There is the law whereby characters may become the servants of their own greedy desires. There is the law wherein a dramatic form of automation takes over which makes each step in a series of actions control the next. So his own choices and options narrow down for Volpone, as they did for Faustus, and then they finally close in upon him, like a Venus's fly-trap.

For there is also the law whereby certain characters may finally become what they had originally intended only to feign. It is 'in our free will' to choose 'what parts we will sustain' in the theatre of the world, or so said Jonson. Thus certain characters in *Volpone* choose their parts freely enough; but they subsequently find themselves quite involuntarily trapped in their roles. What they plan to do, or to give up, only temporarily, they finally have to do, or give up, permanently. Corvino thinks he can lend his wife to Volpone for medicinal purposes only, but he ends by losing both the golden Celia and her golden dowry. Sir Politic gets caught in

[6] Proust, *The Past Recaptured*, p. 1017.

his own tortoise-shell. Volpone himself is most explicitly locked into a role which he once freely chose to play:

> our judgment on thee
> Is that thy substance all be straight confiscate
> To the hospital of the *Incurabili*:
> And since the most was gotten by imposture,
> By feigning lame, gout, palsy, and such diseases,
> Thou art to lie in prison, cramp'd with irons,
> Till thou be'st sick and lame indeed.　　(v. xii. 118–24)

As the vicious characters turn against each other, and, indeed, throughout the play, immoral characters illustrate laws of human experience and psychology from which essentially moral conclusions may be derived. Yet Jonson does not distort the truth in order to make a moral point. Indeed, his amoral, creative energies go into his Volpone, his Mosca, into the vicious and the gulled. By contrast, his virtuous characters, Celia and Bonario, seem almost as pathetic, poetically, as they seem helpless, dramatically. Poor Bonario is given the impossible line 'Forbear, foul ravisher! libidinous swine!', which makes him seem somewhat ridiculous even as he rescues the heroine from a fate worse than death. Celia herself, in effect, at least, seems a paper cut-out of a snow-white swan, almost a parody of the chaste *ingénue*.

The forces of good in this play can never win against Jonson's unforgettable, remarkable, and always dominant images of incurable Greed and Folly. Crime is punished, in *Volpone*, but Jonson lets it punish itself. Celia and Bonario do not triumph by force of virtue, nor do they marry and live happily ever after. Given the corrupt jury, their case could have gone the other way, and so, for a time, it did. Here, as in life, vice may be seen as its own, and possibly its only, punishment, while virtue may be seen as its own, and possibly its only, reward. The only sure reward of doing well, in any age, has been the doing of it. On the other hand, a criminal, like Volpone, had better enjoy his devious doings while he is doing them, because his crime may not pay anything at all in the end. All sorts of tricks, all sorts of games, are played in *Volpone*, but no one in the play emerges as a winner. As Volpone himself insists in the Epilogue, the sole beneficiaries of all the contrivings are the members of Ben Jonson's audience. Thus the immoral character, having been punished by his creator's own moral laws, steps forward, as the chief of Jonson's works, and rightly requests the reward of applause for having so splendidly entertained us with his immoral doings. And of course the audience extends the applause for Volpone to Jonson himself, who, through his glittering, grotesque sinners, has shown us 'things like truth' about certain ways of this world, and thus deserves thanks for a black and gold comedy which is so much more than a piece of moralistic propaganda implying an inevitable triumph of virtue over vice.

In propaganda, truth is contaminated or neglected for the sake of something else, for, say, moral, political, religious, economic, ideological, or personal reasons. Even when it begins in truth, propaganda shoots beyond it, or slants it, in the aggressiveness of its interest; and its sign is a rhetoric of persuasion which is designed to preclude any criticism of its premisses.[7] As opposed to propagandists, poets who are themselves as fundamentally moral as Jonson and Milton do not distort the truth about human experience for the sake of some moralistic design upon the reader. Through the thrusts and counter-thrusts of the amoral, moral, and immoral forces operating within them, their poems constantly provoke thought, never preclude it. This is why their readers have to be so attentive. Indeed, the poems themselves frequently contain within them cautionary examples of the power which poetry shares with propaganda, the power to move its audience to substitute easy solutions, wishful thinking, half-truths, or far-fetched fantasies for a rational recognition of things as they are. The speeches of Face and Subtle, Satan and Comus, are designed to enchant, to captivate the imagination of their victims in such a way as to cause the rational, intellectual, and critical faculties to be suspended. Theirs is the incitement to action rather than thought which is characteristic of propaganda. Yet even as they show it up for what it is, Jonson and Milton themselves display its formidable power.

'Rhetoric', says Milton, 'so ensnares men's minds and so sweetly lures them with her chains that at one moment she can move them to pity, at another she can drive them to hatred, at another she can fire them with warlike passion, and at another lift them up to contempt of death itself.'[8] By playing upon natural and powerful

---

[7] See the discussion of propaganda by Ronald Peacock in *Criticism and Personal Taste* (Oxford, 1972), pp. 43–4.

[8] Milton, Prolusion III, 'Against Scholastic Philosophy', *Complete Poems and Major Prose*, p. 605.

human desires for certain success, for quick solutions, for super-
natural powers, it can persuade human beings to deify girls and
gold, mortal men and minerals. It can even persuade human beings
to bow down before plants. Here is Satan's tribute to the fruit of
an apple-tree:

> O Sacred, Wise, and Wisdom-giving Plant,
> Mother of Science, Now I feel thy Power
> Within me clear, not only to discern
> Things in thir Causes, but to trace the ways
> Of highest Agents, deem'd however wise.
> Queen of this Universe, do not believe
> Those rigid threats of Death; ye shall not Die:
> How should ye? By the Fruit? it gives you Life
> To Knowledge.   (*Paradise Lost*, IX. 679–87)

Convinced of its virtues by Satan, Eve echoes his hymn to the tree:

> O Sovran, virtuous, precious of all Trees
> In Paradise, of operation blest
> To Sapience, hitherto obscur'd, infam'd,
> And thy fair Fruit let hang, as to no end
> Created; but henceforth my early care,
> Not without Song, each Morning, and due praise
> Shall tend thee.   (IX. 795–801)

Though the 'persuasive Rhetoric' that 'sleek'd his tongue, and
won so much on *Eve*' may finally prove useless against his ultimate
adversary (*Paradise Regained*, IV. 1–7), Satan can still boast to his
legions that he caused the Fall of Man and that he did it,

> the more to increase
> Your wonder, with an Apple.   (X. 486–7)

Yet to Eve that apple was not just an apple. It was an 'intellectual fruit' of operation blessed 'to Sapience'. That is, of course,
the way Satan presented it to her. Furthermore, even as he very
effectively exaggerated the virtues of the fruit, he equally effectively
discounted the penalties for tasting it:

> will God incense his ire
> For such a petty Trespass, and not praise
> Rather your dauntless virtue, whom the pain
> Of Death denounc't, whatever thing Death be,
> Deterr'd not from achieving what might lead
> To happier life, knowledge of Good and Evil;

Of good, how just? of evil, if what is evil
Be real, why not known, since easier shunn'd?
God therefore[9] cannot hurt ye, and be just;
Not just, not God; not fear'd then, nor obey'd:
Your fear itself of Death removes the fear.   (IX. 692–702)

All the arts of a great orator are here exploited to ensnare Eve's
mind with persuasive words, 'impregn'd/With Reason, to her
seeming, and with Truth' (IX. 737–8). Satan begins by posing
some interesting and impressive arguments. To attempt to answer
them would, at the very least, require hours and hours of thought:
from a purely rational point of view, the trespass itself *is* petty;
as a symbolic action, it is momentous. So arguments on both sides
could go on and on. And why *not* know evil, since, when known,
it may be easier shunned? How long would it take to answer that
question? Satan's speech thus begins in truth, or at least in
significant half-truths. Then it looses the assault on the will which
is characteristic of propaganda. The line 'Your fear itself of Death
removes the fear' sounds wonderfully convincing and profoundly
true. But what on earth does it mean? The juggling of abstract
concepts, 'good', 'evil', 'justice', 'fear', confuses the intellect.
Sheer repetition gives a formal pattern, an ordered progression to
Satan's phrases. Though there is no logical argument in them,
there is the hypnotic force of a chant or an incantation.[10]

All this is well and good. 'We, the readers' may see through
Satan's speeches, while Eve does not. But who does so on a first
reading? Even on a second reading, does one really want her to

---

[9] Linda Misek tells me that her computer concordance to *Paradise Lost* shows that
the word 'because' rarely appears in the epic, and it is always associated with God.
Satan never uses 'because'. He prefers 'therefore', and for good reason. 'I punished
you because you deserved it' is one kind of statement; 'You hurt me; therefore I will
hurt your children' is a different kind of statement. Satan's logic is flawed by the
post hoc ergo propter hoc fallacy. His word is *ergo*, 'therefore'.

[10] Compare Face's tribute to the 'philosopher's stone':

'Tis a stone,
And not a stone; a spirit, a soul, and a body:
Which if you do dissolve, it is dissolv'd,
If you coagulate, it is coagulated:
If you make it to fly, it flieth.   (II. v. 40–4)

My discussion of Satan's rhetoric, is indebted to, though in disagreement with,
J. H. Summers, *The Muses's Method: An Introduction to 'Paradise Lost'*, especially his
conclusions about the 'guilty' reader; and Stanley Eugene Fish, *Surprised by Sin: The
Reader in 'Paradise Lost'*. I am also here indebted to Frank Kermode, 'Adam Un-
paradised', in *The Living Milton*.

refuse the fruit? By this point in the epic, and especially after multiple readings of it, one knows Satan well enough to be his accomplice, as well as his critic. Furthermore, one knows Eve well enough to be her sympathetic accomplice as well. Possibly we ought to be appalled by our own complicity, surprised by sin, shown up as guilty readers. But are we? What if, even on a twentieth reading, one persistently remains the accomplice, the confidante of Satan and Eve, seeing the situation from their points of view, understanding what they are doing, and why they are doing it, and somehow approving of them in *spite* of the certain knowledge that from an alternative point of view what they are doing is terribly wrong? What then? Possibly we may have it several ways at once: let the 'guilty' reader serve as judge and jury and so condemn himself along with Satan and Eve; let the emotionally engaged reader join them as a fellow rebel, a co-conspirator against a rigid, though benevolently paternalistic, hierarchy; and let the detached reader, if one exists, observe the action as an impartial witness, suspending judgement and identification alike. The individual reader thus remains at liberty to respond freely, according to his own conscience and experience; and indeed his own responses may change in subsequent readings. It therefore seems futile to insist that any one response is the only right one. Still, in two of the three responses described above, the reader's critical and intellectual faculties interact with his emotional responses. And even the most detached reader might agree with the other two that, while certain of Satan's arguments are obviously specious, they nevertheless remain very provocative, potent, and persuasive.

The Devil's own arguments may thus serve to demonstrate that the arguments of poetry, whether specious or valid, markedly differ from other forms of argument in their power to 'move'. The poet, says Sidney, 'yeeldeth to the powers of the minde an image of that whereof the *Philosopher* bestoweth but a wordish description, which doth neither strike, pearce, nor possesse the sight of the soule'.[11] Milton, the poet, and Satan, the propagandist, are alike in their ability to possess the sight of the soul. It is, after all, Milton's poetry which transforms us from spectators into understanders, from judges into accomplices or witnesses, which acts as

11 *The Defence of Poesie* in *The Prose Works of Sir Philip Sidney*, ed. Albert Feuillerat, vol. II (Cambridge, 1963), p. 14.

his own devil's advocate, which enables us to share his own triumphs of poetic inspiration and discovery, and which thus leaves us with a 'new aquist' of 'true experience' from the great event of reading *Paradise Lost*.

'No one questions the inspirational character of musical or poetic invention because the delight and exaltation that go with it somehow communicate themselves to others. Something *travels*: we are carried away.' And, of course, we are also carried away by supreme works of genius, in whatever field they appear: by those works which may reveal a new heaven, or a new earth, or portend a revolution in man's way of thinking about himself. Nevertheless, for the most part, 'scientific discovery is a private event, and the delight that accompanies it, or the despair of finding it illusory, does not travel'. One scientist may get great satisfaction from another's work and admire it deeply; 'it may give him great intellectual pleasure; but it gives him no sense of participation in the discovery, it does not carry him away, and his appreciation of it does not depend on his being carried away. If it were otherwise the inspirational origins of scientific discovery would never have been in doubt.'[12] The origins of creativity in art and science seem nigh identical. The differences lie in the means by which individual discoveries are properly communicated to others, in the nature of the problems considered, and in the tests by which imaginative insights may subsequently be evaluated.

The scientist tackles a problem in order to solve it, and to pass on his solution to others. He may cry 'Eureka!' when he suddenly thinks of a likely solution to his problem, but then he will expose his own conjectural solution to refutation by critical experiment; otherwise, his hypothesis may be refuted by other scientists. He will hope to publish his discovery as soon as possible, for someone else may make the identical discovery within a matter of weeks, days, minutes. Watson and Crick worried that Linus Pauling might beat them to the 'double helix'. Had he done so, he probably would have emerged from the race with the identical helix, the same discovery, or, in due time, someone else would have got

[12] P. B. Medawar, 'Hypothesis and Imagination', in *The Art of The Soluble*, p. 155. Several sections of this book, like my *Likenesses of Truth*, grew out of questions Medawar raised in 'Science and Literature', first published in *Encounter* (Jan. 1969), and reprinted in his *Hope of Progress* (London, 1972), pp. 1–18. I have also here taken points from his review of Watson's account of the race for the 'double helix', pp. 101–9.

it. The problems of an artist are of a different kind. Writing his *Twelfth Night*, or his *King Lear*, Shakespeare did not have to worry that someone else might nip in ahead of him with an identical play. His comic and tragic discoveries are uniquely his own. No one else on earth could have duplicated them, ever.

Furthermore, whereas science, by its nature, deals with the soluble problems of men, the poet, playing God, may confront us with certain insoluble problems, with the built-in deadlocks of life itself. He may focus our attention on the inherent difficulties of a problem, on the truths about human experience implicit in it, but offer us no solution: none whatsoever, anywhere. This is why critical efforts to suggest that there are, or ought to be, or ought to have been, pat solutions to the problems faced by, say, Hamlet, seem so futile. For instance, all those arguments that Hamlet should have 'left vengeance to Heaven' have to deny the facts of life, as well as the facts of the play. Though the Lord claimed that vengeance was his, Stalin murdered millions of people before he finally died—an old man. Macbeth's murders were increasing, in a kind of geometrical progression, before Macduff finally got to him; and Macbeth started out at least as good a man as Claudius. Furthermore, for Hamlet to have behaved like the patient Griselda would have been to violate his own integrity, to refuse to face up to the obvious: there was something rotten in the state of Denmark; the time was out of joint; and, tragically enough, he was born and bound to set things right. Sometimes it may be an act of virtue to forgo revenge; sometimes the interests of justice may require revenge. Sometimes people may be damned if they do, and just as surely damned if they don't. Sometimes life offers no midway between equally horrible alternatives: 'To be, or not to be?' Which would be worse?

'Damned if I do, and damned if I don't.' 'Heads he wins, tails I lose.' These are clichés. Yet when reading *Hamlet*, they are apprehended as facts and problems of human experience which, like the Prince of Denmark, we may all sometimes face. This is one reason why *Hamlet* has survived, while, say, Davenant's *Love and Honour* has not. Throughout his tragedy, Shakespeare captivates the mind by recollection and by curiosity, by reviving natural sentiments and impressing new appearances of things, by awakening those ideas that slumber in the heart. By contrast, the problems posed in Davenant's play are paper-problems faced by wooden things upon wires. In *Phèdre* the conflict between 'love and honour' itself becomes a genuine clash between mighty opposites, an active combat; so, like Shakespeare's, Racine's play has stood the test of time. The 'illusions' have stayed.

The assaults made on art by time are severe; survival is the rare exception, not the general rule, and continuing survival is never guaranteed. The poem or play must face new tests with every new generation. It will be required to do different things, to speak in different ways, by every individual who reads or sees it. For the individual reader is the monitor of the tests of time and truth, and the cumulative verdict, arrived at quite independently by very different individuals, by very different generations, will determine the fate of the individual poem.

That verdict is often based on whether, like *Love and Honour*, the work bores us with its truisms; or whether, like *Hamlet*, it disturbs and enlightens us with its truth. The crucial difference between them lies in the way various truths, which themselves may be abbreviated as truisms ('this above all, to thine own self be true'), are arrived at by the poet and transmitted to us: 'As for the truths which the intelligence—even that of the finest minds— garners right out in the open, . . . their value may be very great, . . . but they have not been recreated'.[13] It is thus that a proverbial or philosophical truism, like 'virtue is its own reward', may be transformed, by different poets, into poetic truth, and so felt as a discovered truth, not a truism, by members of an audience at, say, *The Duchess of Malfi* or *King Lear*.[14] Reading *Paradise Lost* thus markedly differs from reading *The Christine Doctrine* or the *Areopagitica*, though it shares many of the same ideas. For in *Paradise Lost* the ideas are re-enacted, re-created, brought to sensuous and passionate life, and so felt upon the pulses, rediscovered afresh, in subsequent readings. Admirers of *Paradise Lost*, *Hamlet*, *Troilus and Criseyde*, or *Remembrance of Things Past* can turn to them over and over again, as sources of personal discovery. When discoveries cease, re-readings stop, but certain works seem inexhaustible.

It may be, as E. H. Gombrich has argued, that a primary source

---

[13] Proust, *The Past Recaptured*, p. 1015. They are 'all on the surface, with no depth, because no depths had to be penetrated in order to get to them'.

[14] The chief moral of *King Lear*, as George Orwell saw it, was that 'if you live for others, you must live *for others*, and not as a roundabout way of getting an advantage for yourself'. For further discussion of 'survival', see Frank Kermode, 'The Patience of Shakespeare' and 'The Survival of the Classic', in *Renaissance Essays* (London, 1971).

of enjoyment comes from our active participation in the artistic processes of re-creation and discovery: 'we enjoy nothing more than the demand made on us to exercise our own . . . imagination and thus to share in the creative adventure of the artist'.[15] There are, of course, many ways in which the poet may elicit one's imaginative co-operation. Shakespeare, for instance, may raise questions about the past or future experiences of his characters which serve to bring them to life in our minds, since we have to supply answers to them for ourselves. The technique is most obvious in *Hamlet*, but it occurs with some frequency throughout his works. Under what circumstances was Shylock, 'as a bachelor', given a ring by 'Leah'? Who was Leah? Was she Jessica's mother? And what happened to her? The circumstantial detail provided here differs markedly from, say, Barabas's famous recollection, 'I have committed fornication, but that was in another country, and besides the wench is dead'. The method is essentially the same, but the emphasis on intimate detail is characteristic of Shakespeare. Lady Macbeth tells us that she has known what it is like to *nurse* a child, and that Duncan resembled her own father as he slept. Whatever happened to her father, and how many children had Lady Macbeth? Several rings are given to bachelors in *The Merchant of Venice*; numerous parents and children are referred to in *Macbeth*. Thus it is not altogether madness to wonder about the child Lady Macbeth once nursed, about that special ring which Shylock would not have traded for a wilderness of monkeys. Perhaps we are supposed to wonder.

At the turn of the century, it was fashionable to talk about Shakespeare's characters as if they were real people. Scholars asked questions about the girlhood of Shakespeare's heroines, and wondered what subjects Hamlet once studied at Wittenberg. Since then, scholarly and critical prohibitions have been imposed upon such practices; indeed, speculations of this kind have been effectively forbidden. What was yesterday's fashion is today's taboo. Yet the phenomenon itself was an interesting and significant one, and may represent a natural response to Shakespeare's method of bringing certain characters to life in the mind of an audience. As anyone teaching knows, students have to be taught *not* to raise questions about, say, Shylock's past.[16] Why such

---

15 *Art and Illusion*, p. 236.
16 See William Empson, *Milton's God*, p. 69. 'There was a fashion', he says, 'for

natural speculation should be forbidden at the same time that articles asking 'What Kind of Pre-Contract Had Angelo?' regularly appear in the most reputable scholarly journals is itself an interesting question.[17] One might learn a lot from studying critical taboos and vogues of various kinds. But the point here is that, while Shakespeare never once, in the text of *Measure for Measure*, suggests that there was any significant difference between Claudio's pre-contract and Angelo's,[18] he does, in fact, himself bring up Shylock's Leah. Indeed, he seems to have been aware, from the very beginning of his career, of the kind of appeals that could be made to the imagination of an audience by way of

---

attacking "character-analysis", especially in Shakespeare, which I have taken some time to get out of; maybe it has a kind of truth, but it is dangerously liable to make us miss points of character.' See also Gombrich, *Meditations on a Hobby Horse* (London, 1971), p. 146: 'All education, after all, starts with *don'ts*. We first learn what to avoid if we are not to disgrace ourselves in public. In matters of behaviour this is as it should be. In matters of art it leads to an unthinking acceptance of mere taboos. These fashionable *don'ts* are so easily picked up.'

[17] Questions of this kind, as opposed to unanswerable questions about Lady Macbeth's children, are respectable nowadays, because it might be possible, by ransacking Elizabethan records, to answer them. But researchers into Elizabethan documents may well arrive at opposite conclusions. For instance, the argument that the two crucial pre-contracts in *Measure for Measure* were both *de praesenti* betrothals has been countered by the argument that the contract between Angelo and Mariana was a *de futuro* betrothal; and this conclusion, in turn, has been challenged by the argument that the contract between Claudio and Julietta was a *de futuro* betrothal. See Davis P. Harding, 'Elizabethan Betrothals and *Measure for Measure*', *JEGP*, 49 (1950), 139–58; Ernest Schanzer, 'The Marriage-Contracts in *Measure for Measure*', *Shakespeare Survey*, 13 (1960), 81–9, and S. Nagarajan, '*Measure for Measure* and Elizabethan Betrothals', *Shakespeare Quarterly*, 14 (1963), 115–19. Rejecting all these arguments, A. L. French (*Shakespeare and the Critics*, p. 17) asserts that Claudio had no pre-contract at all; that he was lying when he told Lucio that he had a 'true contract' with Julietta, 'who was fast his wife'. French thus softens us up for his later argument that Kent and Cordelia were probably lying when they said that Goneril and Regan threw King Lear out into the storm (p. 154). 'Anything goes', people once thought, so far as discussion about Lady Macbeth's progeny was concerned; and, so far as interpretations of Shakespeare's plays are concerned, anything still goes. One wonders how many of our interpretations will survive beyond the decades in which the scholarly, or critical, vogue they represent is dominant.

[18] I have elsewhere argued that the wheels of the action of *Measure for Measure* turn full circle in order to make certain that Angelo will offend against the law of Vienna in exactly the same way that Claudio did. Furthermore, to argue that 'the Eizabethans' would have made radical moral distinctions between what Angelo did with Mariana and what Claudio did with Julietta, on account of some super-subtle distinctions between pre-contracts is, in effect, to accuse them of a legalism as rigid and unfeeling as Angelo's. See my note, 'What Kind of Pre-Contract had Angelo?', *College English*, 36 (1974), 173–9.

abbreviated information. 'For much imaginary work was there',
he says, as he describes a painting of the Fall of Troy:

> That for Achilles' image stood his spear,
> Griped in an armed hand; himself, behind,
> Was left unseen, save to the eye of mind:
> A hand, a foot, a face, a leg, a head,
> Stood for the whole to be imagined.
>
> (*The Rape of Lucrece*, 1421–7)

Throughout his career, Shakespeare transcribes this kind of visual
shorthand into dramatic terms. He leaves things unseen, save to
the eye of mind, and knows what can stand for the whole to be
imagined. So does Chaucer.

Like Shakespeare, Chaucer knows exactly how much to tell us,
how much to leave to the imagination. For instance, he supplies
his audience with the following information about the Wife of
Bath's looks: she had a bold, fair face that was red of hue, and she
had broad hips. She was gap-toothed. She wore a huge hat, scarlet
stockings, new shoes, and spurs. Given the strikingly vivid
impression made by the description, this seems sparse information
about what she actually looked like.[19] Yet this is all Chaucer
says, or needs to say. Since we come to know her personality so
well, we can supply the colour of her hair, her eyes, her other
clothes, for ourselves, and thus recognize her anywhere and
everywhere: on tours; on ships; at weddings, and, of course, at
funerals; in bars and pubs and restaurants; wherever she might
turn up in her manifold and eternal returns. For Chaucer to have
typed her, for all eternity, as, say, a brunette, would have denied
us the pleasure of recognizing her in her blonde and red-headed
manifestations as she wanders on, in her continuing travels, with,
or without, that sixth husband.

Through her own Prologue and Tale, we are effectively transformed into Dame Alice's 'gossips'; and indeed we may, in turn,
gossip about her with each other. Did she ever catch her sixth

---

[19] Chaucer gives us no specific details about the way Griselda and Walter looked.
His interest in them is in their situation. And we recognize their modern counterparts by their situation, not their looks. When Chaucer directs an appeal to the moral
judgement, as he does in *The Clerk's Tale*, he tends to stylize his characters. To have
characterized Walter as richly as he does the Wife, or the Pardoner, would be to have
our judgement suspended by fascination with him as an individual. Chaucer thus is
careful to define Walter, just as Walter defines Griselda, solely in terms of the relationship between Power and Patience, tyrant and victim.

husband? Was she claiming triumph or admitting defeat when she
told us that she had 'had the world as in her time'? Did she mean,
in effect, that she is the ultimate winner, who can for ever say,
'Tomorrow do thy worst/For I have lived today'? Or is she more
resigned, more nostalgic, like Shaw's Caesar, who can, at least,
say goodbye to youth without useless complaints or undue regret:
'I am an old man—worn out now—true, quite true. . . . Well,
every dog has his day; and I have had mine: I cannot complain.'
Or do her lines represent a lament, do they spring out of a profound depression and fear for the future, when she will have to
sell chaff rather than grain, with ever more effort and ever less
profit? Or do the lines simply indicate that she will show a
continual and commendable valour in the war-games of love, that
she is a kind of sexual counterpart, a comic equivalent, to Words-
worth's heroic Leech-Gatherer? Does the fact that she had no
children (apart from literary ones) mark her as having missed her
true vocation in life, or as having found it and, indeed, managed
her affairs very well? She never mentions children among the
things women most desire, and might have agreed with Scarlett
O'Hara, who herself had three husbands, that 'no woman in her
right mind would have any children if she could help it'. The
individual reader thus becomes the accomplice of Chaucer himself,
aiding and abetting his schemes, as his own imaginative and
emotional responses to her interact with Chaucer's in the process
of creating the Wife of Bath who will travel along, in the individual memory, for ever after.

   Somewhere in *Joseph Andrews*, Fielding inserts a vacant line,
following the description of some lovely young miss, so that the
reader can write in the name of his beloved, and thus put his own
sweetheart into Fielding's novel, even as he fills out the details of
Fielding's description in his own imagination. And indeed, 'we
can never read a novel', said Proust, 'without giving its heroine
the form and features of the woman with whom we are in love'.[20]
It certainly may be true that the closest most people ever come to
being poets is when they are in love.

   Whereas our imaginations are usually devoted to ourselves—
to dressing-up, gilding, blackening, censoring, and otherwise
tinkering with our own fictions about ourselves—questions about
the beloved will suggest all sorts of fictions about someone else.

[20] Proust, *The Sweet Cheat Gone*, p. 699.

The jealous lover will give his beloved all sorts of horrible, or interesting, vices; the romantic lover will endow his sweetheart with the divine beauty of a Helen, the divine variety of a Cleopatra. Precisely like that of the poet, the imagination of the lover creates its own 'characters of love', and makes up stories about them.

> *Cleopatra.* Where think'st thou he is now? Stands he, or sits he?
> Or does he walk? or is he on his horse?
> O happy horse, to bear the weight of Antony!
> Do bravely, horse! for wot'st thou whom thou movest?
> The demi-Atlas of this earth, the arm
> And burgonet of men. He's speaking now,
> Or murmuring 'Where's my serpent of old Nile?'
>   (*Antony and Cleopatra*, I. v. 19–25)

When one is in love, the imagination, anticipation, memory, and desire centre around another person. Like a writer creating a character, the lover will ask questions of his imagination, and his imagination, like that of an artist, will supply the answers. Thus, as Shakespeare reminds us in *A Midsummer Night's Dream*, the lover and the poet alike may make lunatic mistakes.

Similar problems do indeed confront people in their aesthetic and intellectual bursts of creative inspiration and in the experience of love; for in all such highly charged situations 'the external validation of the experience' may not correlate with its 'phenomenological self-validation'. What we thought was a bear may turn out to be only a bush. It is possible for the great insight to be mistaken, the great love to disappear, while 'the poem that creates itself in a peak-experience may have to be thrown away later as unsatisfactory'.[21] Like an experience of love, the intellectual insight, the poetic vision, may prove to be 'the tricks of strong imagination', of juggling fiends, of one's own deluding devils that can, upon occasion, assume the pleasing shape of the divine, the unique, the transcendent Helen-of-inspiration who can make mortals immortal with a single kiss.

The essential difficulty, the nigh-insoluble problem here, is that the moment of insight, the creation of a poem, or the experience of a passionate love which will indeed stand up to the tests of time and truth 'feels subjectively the same' as the creation of a product,

[21] A. H. Maslow, 'Cognition of Being in the Peak-Experiences', in *Towards a Psychology of Being* (Princeton, N.J., 1962), p. 94.

or some experience of love, that will not stand such tests—and vice versa.[22] Under the influence of Cupid's flower, Lysander felt as unequivocally devoted to his new love, Helena, as he did to his true love, Hermia. Likewise, one can never be certain that one's own critical insights are not mistaken. The imagination, facing products of the imagination, will respond as it will, and the reasoning intelligence will be put to work to prove true whatever the imagination wishes to believe true of the work to which it has responded, or failed to respond. The history of criticism teems with efforts to provide tests by which imaginative responses to works of art may be validated. But the moment the powers of reason and intelligence try to judge and explain works of the imagination, there is nothing fixed or certain for them to go by, apart from the works themselves; and, as we have seen, different, and, indeed, diametrically opposite, conclusions can easily be drawn from the evidence supplied within an individual work. Thus desperate efforts have been made to supply some external criteria of judgement, some guideline to the 'proper' responses. For instance, in recent years a sustained effort has been made to recapture, from shreds and patches of information, the imaginative and moral responses of a long-dead contemporary audience to, say, the imaginary beings created by Chaucer and Shakespeare. But, here again, one can prove well-nigh anything one wishes to prove about the original audience: the same audience that 'would have' disapproved of, say, Falstaff, flocked to see him. The quest for certainty in criticism, as Keats said it was in poetry, as Popper says it is for science, and as it always is in love, may be futile. The only sure test, as Dr. Johnson recognized, is the test of time, which, so far as literature is concerned, is the best test of truth.

Indeed, the poet himself may, if he chooses, remind us of the uncertain nature of human certainties. In doing so, he may give

[22] Maslow, *Towards a Psychology of Being*, p. 94; 'The habitually creative person knows this well, expecting half of his great moments of insight not to work out.' The great work 'needs not only the flash, the inspiration, the peak-experience; it also needs hard work, long training, unrelenting criticism, perfectionistic standards. . . . Now come the questions, "Is it true?" "Will it be understood by the other?" "Is its structure sound?" "Does it stand the test of logic?" "How will it do in the world?" "Can I prove it?" Now come the comparisons, the judgments, the evaluations, the cold, morning after thoughts, the selections and the rejections . . . That creativity which uses *both* types of process easily and well, in good fusion or in good succession, I shall call "Integrated creativity". It is from this kind that comes the great work of art, or philosophy or science' (p. 134).

immortality to the mistaken insights of a Leontes (who thought
he had seen a spider that was not there), or to the false love of a
Troilus, as well as to genuine insights and marriages of true
minds. Sometimes he may affirm the value of the uncertainties of
human love and life, of the foul rag-and-bone shop of the heart,
even over the purged images of pure art. Certain works of art
themselves remind us that, though art is superhuman in that it may
survive and transcend its mortal makers and models, it yet falls
short of the truly living, and therefore only mortal, works of God:
no chisel ever yet cut breath.

It is only in art, only in the imagination, that the poet can call
back yesterday and raise the dead to life again:

> Methought I saw my late espoused Saint
>> Brought to me like *Alcestis* from the grave,
>> Whom *Jove's* great Son to her glad Husband gave,
>> Rescu'd from death by force though pale and faint.
>
> . . . .
>
> Her face was veil'd, yet to my fancied sight,
> Love, sweetness, goodness, in her person shin'd
> So clear, as in no face with more delight.
>> But O, as to embrace me she inclin'd,
>> I wak'd, she fled, and day brought back my night.
>>>> (Milton, Sonnet XXIII)

The greatest poet in the world cannot command the forces of
nature to make his personal dreams come true, his illusions stay;
he can only summon shadows.

In Lyly's *Campaspe*, the artist, Apelles, is commissioned by
Alexander to paint a portrait of the beautiful captive, Campaspe.
The living woman is to be transformed, by the painter's art, into
the goddess Venus. Before he saw Campaspe, Apelles had been
unable to finish the face of his goddess, but Alexander tells him
that, when he sees her, the painter will find 'finished by nature'
what he has been 'trifling about by art'. And Apelles admits that
'in absolute beauty there is somewhat above art'. Then, even as
the work of nature completes the work of art, the man, Apelles,
falls in love with the woman, Campaspe.

Campaspe. Whom do you honour most, Apelles?
Apelles. The thing that is likest you, Campaspe.
Campaspe. My picture?
Apelles. I dare not venture upon your person. (IV. ii. 49–51)

'O, Campaspe, Campaspe!', he says; 'Art must yield to nature, reason to appetite, wisdom to affection.' There are regions of human emotion that lie beyond the control of the intellect or of art: 'Now must I paint things unpossible for mine art but agreeable with my affections: deep and hollow sighs, sad and melancholy thoughts.'

Before he finally wins Campaspe herself, Apelles recognizes that only in his imagination may the miracle of Pygmalion come true:

> *Apelles.* Then will I gaze continually on thy picture.
> *Campaspe.* That will not feed thy heart.
> *Apelles.* Yet shall it fill mine eye! Besides, the sweet thoughts, the sure hopes, thy protested faith, will cause me to embrace thy shadow continually in mine arms, of the which, by strong imagination, I will make a substance. (IV. iv. 12–18)

But only by 'strong imagination'; through his own imagination and art, Apelles will come as close as he possibly can to the substance, the living reality. He remains fully aware that his dream will ever fall short of the reality itself. This explains why 'A moment of complete happiness never occurs in the creation of a work of art. The promise of it is felt in the act of creation, but disappears towards the completion of the work. For it is then that the painter realizes that it is only a picture he is painting. Until then he had almost dared to hope that the picture might spring to life.'[23]

And while Shakespeare manages, as successfully as any human being can, to seize, to grasp, to possess, and so exhibit before us, his visions of beauty, love, evil, and folly, he also constantly suggests that the living human being remains 'somewhat above art' and 'past the size of dreaming'. If there ever were a man such as Antony, Cleopatra insists, he must have been a product of nature, and not some shadow-man of her imagination:

> nature wants stuff
> To vie strange forms with fancy; yet to imagine
> An Antony, were nature's piece 'gainst fancy,
> Condemning shadows quite. (V. ii. 97–100)

Shakespeare, in turn, insists that the living Cleopatra, going to meet her Antony on the river Cydnus, was superior to any work

[23] Lucien Freud, quoted by Gombrich, *Art and Illusion*, p. 80.

of art, as she lay in her pavilion, 'O'er-picturing that Venus where we see/The fancy outwork nature'. And indeed, the natural world itself seems diminished when Shakespeare's ageing, flawed, and mortal Antony and Cleopatra go to join Dido and Aeneas in that other world of fables, songs, and fleeting shades.

Flawed, vulnerable, and mortal though they may be, living human beings are, in Shakespeare, consistently held to be superior to any mere shadows of the imagination. Thus the living Ferdinand and Miranda, laughing and playing a game of chess, are themselves the 'most high miracle' brought forth by Prospero. In *The Winter's Tale*, the dream of Orpheus and the dream of Pygmalion both come true when the statue of Hermione turns out to be Hermione herself. Leontes believes that he is 'mocked with art', but, at the command of Paulina, his 'late espoused saint' is in fact recalled to life, rescued from death:

Paulina.   Music, awake her; strike!
    'Tis time; descend; be stone no more; approach;
    Strike all that look upon with marvel. Come,
    I'll fill your grave up: stir, nay, come away,
    Bequeath to death your numbness, for from him
    Dear life redeems you.   (v. iii. 98–103)

What appeared, at first, to be a perfect work of art turns out to be life itself. Watching the statue-scene, it is as if one watches that miraculous moment when the respiration becomes regular, the pulse rate returns to normal, the eyes open, and the lips move. Paulina's art, like Shakespeare's, so glorifies the wonder-working, life-giving, power of nature that when the majestic but 'coldly' standing statue of Hermione is infused with 'warm life' one cannot but marvel at the miracle:

Leontes.   O, she's warm!
    If this be magic, let it be an art
    Lawful as eating.
Polixenes.   She embraces him.
Camillo. She hangs about his neck.   (v. iii. 109–12)

In Shakespeare, the experience of human love competes with and, indeed, finally wins over life itself as the greatest wonder, the most high miracle, the final mystery. Love lost, destroyed, thrown away, squandered on unworthy objects, and, sometimes, regained has been the subject of several works discussed here.

Shakespeare's plays remind us that love can move men to transcendent acts of unselfishness, drive them to murder, fire them with
passion, make the dead live, and lift the living up to contempt of
death itself. Of course, like poetry, love may be a primary source
of error, but, like poetry, it may also reveal truth. In its highest
form, its authentic form, it is always a manifestation of freedom,
for it must be mutually and freely given and received:

Cleopatra.	Husband, I come:
	Now to that name my courage prove my title! (v. ii. 290–1)
Romeo.	I pray thee, chide not: she whom I love now
	Doth grace for grace and love for love allow. (II. iii. 85–6)

'In our will to love or not,' says Milton, 'In this we stand or fall'.
It is love which breaks down the barriers between nature and art,
comedy and tragedy, life and death, in *The Winter's Tale*, and it was
the will to love which broke the deadlock between Adam and Eve
and so makes them 'precious winners' too, even though they lost
their original Paradise.

Of course these works emphasize the dangers of love, just as
they emphasize its miraculous powers. But they also suggest that
to deny love is to deny life. To fear to err, in this sense, is to fall
into the worst error of all. In the real world, as in the world of art,
what finally counts may be the will to love, to try, to make the
search, to make the wild surmise, to take the risks:

It is possible that in order to keep love, feeling, tenderness alive, it
will be necessary to feel these emotions ambiguously, even for what is
false and debased, or for what is still an idea, a shadow in the willed
imagination only . . . or if what we feel is pain, then we must feel it,
acknowledging that the alternative is death. Better anything than the
shrewd, the calculated, the non-committal, the refusal of giving for fear
of the consequences.[24]

By this standard, better to be Cleopatra, or Antony, or Enobarbus,
than Octavius. Better, before death takes us, to be a truly human
being who has 'sighed deep, laughed free, starved, feasted, des-
paired—been happy', and so have truly lived, than to be Augustus
Caesar. ''Tis paltry to be Caesar', as he is here presented. For
though he wins his empire, Shakespeare's cautious, calculating,
politic Octavius seems like one of Ibsen's 'trolls' who adopt the
motto 'To thyself be Enough' in eternal opposition to human

24 Doris Lessing, *The Golden Notebook*, p. 467.

beings, like Cleopatra, who to themselves are true. Indeed, in the end, Shakespeare's 'lass unparallel'd' proves Caesar to be an 'ass unpolicied' by exacting from him the tribute he had once hoped to exact from her. She will never march in his triumph; he will have to march in hers. He wins quite enough, but Cleopatra would never have settled for that.

Thus, if by his standards, he wins and she loses; she wins and he loses by hers. And so, like Antony, Enobarbus, Octavia, and Charmian, we finally have to decide for ourselves which side we will join forces with; to which we will give our admiration; in which of their triumphs, and under which standard, we ourselves will march. For whereas, from one point of view, the argument of tragedy is that it is better, because safer, to be a shrub rather than an oak,[25] to be 'Type B' rather than 'Type A', to be Octavius rather than Cleopatra, from another point of view, the lesson of tragedy, and, perhaps, of life itself, may be precisely the opposite. For that matter, certain losers in literature and life alike effectively remind us that there is no safety; that death evens all our odds; that shrewd Caesar, too, will die and turn to clay; that shrubs as well as oaks, ordinary people as well as remarkable ones, may be blasted by the lightning.

Fearing the impending battle between the forces of Antony and Caesar, Octavia was distressed that she could find 'no midway/ 'Twixt these extremes at all'. Like many people, Octavia would prefer a middle way through life; and, indeed, she represents one. Her rival, Cleopatra, herself rejects, and represents the rejection of, the middle ground, the crowded *via media*. In her, opposites usually held to be in hostile conflict come together and dance and embrace. Art and nature, biology and imagination, falsehood and truth, genuine passion and consummate acting all fuse in her poetry,

---

[25] See Helen Gardner, *Religion and Literature*, p. 21: 'Some have held that tragedies exist to impress on us the same lesson: be moderate, observe the mean, be well balanced, normal and inoffensive. The wind strikes the lofty tree: it passes harmlessly over the lowly shrub. Be a shrub: see what happens to trees. The personages of tragedy are, in this view, warnings to us, examples of pride, arrogance, obstinacy, and of failures to understand their own natures and the nature of the world. We may learn from these "over-reachers" to bear ourselves modestly and humbly, recognize the limitations of our human condition, and make no great demands upon life'. It is, says A. H. Maslow, 'the god-like in ourselves' and in other human beings, that we are most ambivalent about, fascinated by and fearful of, motivated to and defensive against. This is why we may deny our talents, our finest impulses, our highest potentialities, in the struggle against our own *hubris*. *Towards a Psychology of Being*, p. 58.

her personality, and her behaviour. She thus is always remarkable, never ordinary. And whereas the self-effacing, gentle, compliant, and domestic Octavia may be, by conventional standards, an ideal wife, Cleopatra can be all those things to Antony that Octavia neither could nor would dare to be. She is his harlot, and his queen; his serpent of Old Nile, and his terrene Isis. She sometimes puts on his 'sword Philippan'; she laughs at him; goes fishing with him; starts fights with him; comforts him; drinks him to his bed. And thus her union with him, in life and death, represents that marriage of true minds which will not admit impediment.[26] As indeed the middle range of human experience necessarily must be, Octavia's range is narrowly limited; neither in nature nor in art can she compete with Cleopatra, whose range extends from elemental extreme to elemental extreme.

Indeed, Cleopatra represents a fusion of art with nature unprecedented in Shakespearian tragedy. The word 'art', which occurs so frequently in the comedies and romances, is virtually absent from the tragedies, perhaps by necessity. For 'art' involves an attempt to control nature, or, at least, to refine it. It implies man's ability to impose his own design upon life. Tragedy concerns nature out of order, beyond human control. Cleopatra, both artist and *objet d'art*, is eulogized as such throughout the play. Her charms are never overthrown, she never abandons her art, and she dies, looking like a masterpiece, of her own design. Yet Shakespeare here, as always, affirms the desirability of life. For he constantly insists that the earthy, vital, varied Cleopatra was infinitely more wonderful than any changeless work of art, any fleeting shade of the imagination. While she lived, it was as if nature itself was sustaining Shakespeare's art, as well as her own; and as if this product of his art had an independent life of her own. It was when she drank of Egypt's grape, when she was earth and water, as well as fire and air, that she was his living masterpiece. In her death-scene, the processes of Hermione's resurrection are reversed. The miracle occurred when the statue turned into

---

[26] *Enobarbus.* Octavia is of a holy, cold, and still conversation.
    Menas. Who would not have his wife so?
    Enobarbus. Not he that himself is not so; which is Mark Antony. . . . Antony
    will use his affection where it is: he married but his occasion here.
                                             (II. vi. 130–9)
My discussion here is specially (and obviously) indebted to A. C. Bradley, 'Antony and Cleopatra', *Oxford Lectures on Poetry* (London, 1920), pp. 279–308.

'blessed matter', when nature infused art with life. And the tragedy occurs when the passionate woman appears as a cold, majestic statue, when art takes leave of life. Life will go on without art, and so Caesar's world goes on after Cleopatra's death. Its range is, none the less, diminished by her absence. She leaves a gap in nature when she goes.[27]

As for Cleopatra, she will join Antony to act again, before some other audience, where troops of admirers, forsaking Dido and Aeneas, will be theirs. And it does not seem to matter whether their show will go on in the infernal regions or in the empyrean ones. For they are representative of those exceptional individuals, those chief works of God and man, who sometimes emerge in life and literature, and of whom one must say, as Antony and Cleopatra say of each other, 'Whatever your frailties and follies may have been, you made the world around you more remarkable, enjoyable, exciting, amusing, noble, and grand by being in it, and the only after-life worth going to will be the one where you are':

> Without you, Heaven would be too dull to bear,
> And Hell will not be Hell if you are there.[28]

And in retrospect, what of those others, of Juliet and King Lear, De Flores, and even Griselda, of all those others to whom kingdoms were but clay in comparison with their love? 'What need'st thou with thy tribe's black tents', asks the Arabian love-song, 'Who hast the red pavilion of my heart?' For such characters, this is a rhetorical question to be answered in the negative. And however romantic or heroic, base or sublime, their individual claims to enter the red pavilions may be, it seems finally fitting—though not, of course, altogether just—that those who longed for love and somehow won it should come, if only now and again, into their reward.

---

[27] It does not seem very consoling to conclude, however smugly, that, after all, one will survive her departure and that Octavius, and the ways of our world which he represents, will also survive. Indeed we may, at the end, look upon Caesar's world with a trace of contempt, and finally walk out on Caesar himself, dismissing him as not worth our own leave-taking.

[28] The couplet is from John Sparrow's tribute to Maurice Bowra, in *Maurice Bowra: A Celebration*, ed. Hugh Lloyd-Jones (London, 1974), p. 155.

Index

Authors and their works are indexed separately.